Grill Cookbook For Be

Mastering the Art of Grilling with 100 Easy and Tasty

Recipes

ANTHONY TAYLOR

Your Free Gift

As a way of saying thanks for your purchase, to our readers we offer as a gift a printable recipe book, to download for free: "Cookbook Journal", a diary in which to keep track of all your culinary inventions, assigning each one an evaluation, the difficulty of execution and much more.

Click this link to free download https://dl.bookfunnel.com/i3sq7ljm6z

Contents

Introduction

Grilling is a type of cooking that involves the application of dry heat to all sides of food, typically from the top, bottom, or sides. This method is often used to cook meat and vegetables.

Many types of grills that are available in the market, with the cheapest typically being a small $20 charcoal grill and the more expensive ones reaching $15,000. Nonetheless, the basics never change and as long as you keep practicing, your grilling skills will continue to improve as you will eventually master this practice.

There are a few rules you must observe while cooking. First, always keep the grill clean to prevent food from sticking to it. Give yourself some time before starting to cook to clean and properly heat your grill. You should also make sure to keep an eye on what you are grilling at all times and refrain from using any spray water bottle to avoid getting burned. It's also a good idea to remove any excess fat and clean your meat to decrease the amount of fat that drips into your fire.

Grills can become quite hot and easily burn your food. As such, make sure that you check the required temperature as many foods, including chicken, fish, green vegetables, and fruits, are best grilled at low temperatures.

To better control the temperature of your grill, use the dials to decrease the temperature. However, if you are using a charcoal grill, you can also test the temperature with your hands as the longer you can keep your hand over the grill, the lower the temperature is. A popular grilling misconception is that grilled items should not be turned multiple times. However, if you want to flip your food, you should, just make sure that it cooks evenly from all sides.

You should also evenly distribute the food you are cooking over the surface of the grill to decrease the likelihood of the fire flaring up. However, don't panic if this happens as it is still normal for this to take place every now and then.

Even though there are general guidelines on the amount of time it takes to grill food, it is still difficult for some people to determine when the food is completely cooked. There are a few main rules. One is that it is better to slightly overcook your food rather than undercook it, which can be dangerous, especially in the case of meat or poultry. Another rule is that you should verify that the food is fully cooked, such as by using a thermometer to check the internal temperature of the food.

The most significant advantage of having a gas grill is your ability to easily increase or decrease the temperature with a button or knob. You should also read the manual on how to use your particular grill model. For example, these are some of the basic instructions you can follow, if you have just bought a new grill:

- Uncover your grill and clean the surface. Then, turn on the gas supply.
- Wait for the grill to heat up, which should take around 10 minutes as a grill must be hot before it is used.
- Put the food on the hot grill and allow it to cook.
- Flip occasionally when needed.
- Remove the food from the heat when it's fully cooked.
- Turn off the valves.
- Once the grill has cooled down, clean the surface.
- Cover it once again and store it elsewhere.

Charcoal grilling is an art that can take some time to get accustomed to. While it doesn't cook meat or vegetables at an exactly consistent temperature, charcoal grilling can provide you with a more "authentic" experience.

As such, it is key to control the heat by creating a fire, controlling the airflow, and retaining the lid. Hence, practice is key to mastering this art. Some things you should consider while cooking over a charcoal grill are:

- Always keep your grill clean because ashes and waste can get stuck in the vents and result in poor temperature control.

- Ensure that your vents work properly as it is challenging to adjust any rusted or damaged vents.

- Wear a pair of heat-resistant gloves to prevent yourself from being burned.

- Purchase a fire starter to make a fire or use a (charcoal) chimney. Put your grill in a secure and proper position to avoid any accidents.

- Keep your grilling tools nearby, including a strong grill stick to move any burning coals.

In order to start a charcoal fire, there are a few techniques you can follow:

- Ignite the coal and then distribute it evenly.

- Wait 12 to 15 minutes for the charcoal to become hot.

- Once the charcoal is ready, it should look white or dark grey, which indicates that it is very hot from all sides.

- Scatter the charcoal and prepare a single layer of coals to have a medium-sized fire ready.

- Place two layers of charcoal in your grill if you want to attain a higher temperature.

- If you want to cook using indirect heat, then scatter the coals on one side. Then, cook your food on the other side of the grill.

Now that you know the basics of how to grill food, read on to discover how to prepare the recipes we have specified below!

COOKING CONVERSION CHART

Measurement

CUP	ONCES	MILLILITERS	TABLESPOONS
8 cup	64 oz	1895 ml	128
6 cup	48 oz	1420 ml	96
5 cup	40 oz	1180 ml	80
4 cup	32 oz	960 ml	64
2 cup	16 oz	480 ml	32
1 cup	8 oz	240 ml	16
3/4 cup	6 oz	177 ml	12
2/3 cup	5 oz	158 ml	11
1/2 cup	4 oz	118 ml	8
3/8 cup	3 oz	90 ml	6
1/3 cup	2.5 oz	79 ml	5.5
1/4 cup	2 oz	59 ml	4
1/8 cup	1 oz	30 ml	3
1/16 cup	1/2 oz	15 ml	1

Temperature

FAHRENHEIT	CELSIUS
100 °F	37 °C
150 °F	65 °C
200 °F	93 °C
250 °F	121 °C
300 °F	150 °C
325 °F	160 °C
350 °F	180 °C
375 °F	190 °C
400 °F	200 °C
425 °F	220 °C
450 °F	230 °C
500 °F	260 °C
525 °F	274 °C
550 °F	288 °C

Weight

IMPERIAL	METRIC
1/2 oz	15 g
1 oz	29 g
2 oz	57 g
3 oz	85 g
4 oz	113 g
5 oz	141 g
6 oz	170 g
8 oz	227 g
10 oz	283 g
12 oz	340 g
13 oz	369 g
14 oz	397 g
15 oz	425 g
1 lb	453 g

Chapter 1: Grilled Chicken Recipes

1. Grilled Chicken Yucatan Skewers

Preparation Time: 15 min | Serving: 6 | Difficulty Level: Medium

Nutritional Info: Fat: 5g | Carbs: 2g | Protein: 14g

Ingredients

- 6 skinless and boneless chicken thighs

- ½ cup freshly squeezed orange juice

- ¼ cup lime juice

- 2 tbsp. canola oil

- 2 tbsp. ancho chili powder

- 3 cloves of roughly chopped garlic

- 2 tbsp. chipotle

- Salt and black pepper

- Chopped scallions (garnish)

- Grilled lime halves (garnish)

Steps for preparation

1. Place two skewers through each chicken thigh. Then, place the chicken in a large baking dish.

2. Whisk the orange juice, oil, chili powder, lime juice, and garlic together. Pour it onto the thighs and marinate in the refrigerator for 1 to 4 hours.

3. Heat the charcoal grill until the charcoal becomes very hot.

4. Remove the thighs from the marinade and season with salt and pepper.

5. Place the thighs over the grill. Cook them until they become golden brown and are slightly charred, for about 4 minutes per side.

6. Remove the chicken from the grill and let it rest for 5 minutes.

7. Remove the skewers from the chicken and serve with scallions and lime wedges.

2. Spicy Chicken and Grape Skewers

Preparation Time: 10 min | Servings: 4 | Difficulty Level: Easy

Nutritional Info: Fat: 6g | Carbs: 14g | Protein: 27g

Ingredients

- 2 tbsp. olive oil

- ½ tsp of lemon zest

- 1 tbsp. lemon juice

- 2 cloves of minced garlic

- 1 tsp. ground cumin

- ½ tsp. ground coriander

- ½ tsp. salt

- 1 lb. of boneless, skinless, chicken breast, cubed

- 8 wooden skewers

- 1 ½ cups seedless green grapes

- Cooking spray

- 2 tbsp. chopped mint leaves

- 1 lemon wedge

Steps for preparation

1. In a medium-sized bowl, whisk oil, lemon juice, lemon zest, garlic, cumin, salt, and coriander.

2. Add the chicken to the marinade and toss them to coat. Marinate the chicken for 20 minutes. While the chicken marinates, soak the wooden skewers in the water if they are wooden.

3. Thread four pieces of chicken and four grapes onto the skewers, alternating the pieces. Spray the grill pan with the cooking spray and preheat it to medium-high heat.

4. Grill the chicken until it is cooked through, for about 3 to 4 minutes on each side. Sprinkle some mint on top and serve with lemon wedges.

3. Chicken Sate with Ponzu Sauce

Preparation Time: 20 min | Serving: 4 | Difficulty Level: Easy

Nutritional Info: Fat: 3.5g | Carbs: 13.3g | Protein: 39.6g

Ingredients

- 4 chicken breasts

- ¼ cup light brown sugar

- ¼ cup sake (rice wine)

- ¼ cup rice vinegar

- ¼ cup fresh lime juice

- 2 tbsp. soy sauce

- 1 tsp. dark sesame oil

- ¼ tsp. crushed red pepper

- 1 minced garlic clove

- Cooking spray

Steps for preparation

1. Prepare the grill.

2. Cut both chicken breasts lengthwise into four strips. Combine the sugar and remaining ingredients in a small bowl, with the exception of the cooking spray. Then, stir until the sugar dissolves. Proceed to combine half of the mixture with all of the chicken in a large bowl and allow it to marinate for 10 minutes. Then, reserve the remaining sake mixture. Apply some cooking spray to the grill.

3. Drain the chicken and discard the leftover marinade. Then, thread one chicken strip onto a skewer and place it on the heated grill rack. Cook it for 2 minutes until done and serve with the remaining mixture.

4. Spiedini Chicken, Zucchini and Almond Salsa Verde

Preparation Time: 25 min | Serving: 6 | Difficulty Level: Medium

Nutritional Info: Fat: 5.5g | Carbs: 6.3g | Protein: 28.7g

Ingredients

- Salsa

- 1 cup chopped fresh parsley

- 2 tbsp. chopped and toasted almonds

- 2 tbsp. chopped fresh chives

- 3 tbsp. chopped capers

- ½ tsp. grated lemon rind

- 3 tbsp. fresh lemon juice

- 1 tbsp. olive oil

- ½ tsp. chopped fresh thyme

- ½ tsp. chopped fresh oregano

- ¼ tsp. kosher salt

- 1/8 tsp. ground black pepper

- 1 clove of minced garlic

Spiedini:

- 1½ lb. of chicken breasts, cut into pieces

- A small zucchini, cut into 6 slices

- Cooking spray

- ¼ tsp. kosher salt

- 1/8 tsp. black pepper

Steps for preparation

1. Soak twelve (10-inch) wooden skewers in water for 30 minutes to prevent them from burning when on the grill.

2. Preheat the grill so that it is on medium-high heat.

3. Then, to prepare the salsa, combine the first twelve ingredients and set aside.

4. To prepare the spiedini, thread the chicken and zucchini onto each of the twelve (ten-inch) skewers in alternate pieces. Coat the spiedini with the cooking spray and sprinkle salt and pepper onto the skewers. Place them on a grill rack and cook for 6 minutes or until done, turning each skewer once. Serve with salsa.

5. Grilled Watermelon and Balsamic Chicken

Preparation Time: 5 min | Serving: 3 | Difficulty Level: Easy

Nutritional Info: Fat: 12g | Carbs: 27g | Protein: 36g

Ingredients

- 1 lb. of boneless, skinless chicken breasts

- 1 tsp. salt

- ½ tsp. pepper

- 8 1-inch watermelon wedges

- 4 oz. of soft goat cheese

- 6 fresh mint leaves, finely diced

- ¼ cup balsamic vinegar

Steps for preparation

1. Pre-heat the grill. Then, season the chicken breasts with salt and pepper and cook for around 6 to 8 minutes. Add wedges of the watermelon and grill for 1 to 2 minutes on all sides.

2. Remove the chicken and watermelon from the grill. Cut the watermelon into cubes.

3. Top the chicken with watermelon, goat cheese, mint, and balsamic vinegar.

4. Serve immediately.

6. Santa Fe Grilled Chicken Soft Tacos

Preparation Time: 15 min | Serving: 8 | Difficulty Level: Medium

Nutritional Info: Fat: 5g | Carbs: 17g | Protein: 19g

Ingredients

- 2 tbsp. chili powder

- 2 tbsp. cumin

- 1 tbsp. paprika

- ½ tsp. crushed red pepper

- ¼ tsp. salt

- 1/8 tsp. pepper

- 1 tbsp. dark brown sugar

- 2 tbsp. olive oil

- 2 ½ lbs. of skinless chicken breasts

Steps for preparation

1. In a small bowl, combine the chili powder, red pepper, cumin, paprika, salt, pepper and brown sugar. Then, stir in the oil until the mixture is moist but crumbly.

2. Generously rub all sides of the chicken with the chili mixture. Let it marinate for 30 minutes at room temperature (or cover and refrigerate it for up to one day).

3. Preheat the gas grill until it is relatively hot and simultaneously preheat the broiler until it is at a high temperature. Place the rack 6 to 8 inches away from the heat source. Then, grill or broil the chicken until it is firm for about 5 minutes on each side. Let it cool for around 5 minutes and then cut it into thin strips.

4. Finally, warm the tortillas and serve them with the chicken.

7. Grilled Chicken and Tarragon-Dill

Preparation Time: 35 min | Serving: 6 | Difficulty Level: Medium

Nutritional Info: Fat: 22.1g | Carbs: 17.2g | Protein: 19.5g

Ingredients

- ½ cup lemon juice

- ¼ cup olive oil

- 4 garlic cloves, minced

- 1 tbsp. red pepper flakes, crushed

- 3 6-lb. boneless chicken breasts

- ½ cup sour cream

- ½ cup reduced-fat mayonnaise

- ¼ cup cider vinegar or rice vinegar

- ¼ cup fresh lemon juice

- 1 cup seedless red grapes

- 1 large Granny Smith apple

- ½ cup diced celery

- ½ cup finely chopped onion

- ½ cup finely chopped fresh tarragon

- 2 tbsp. fresh dill, finely chopped

- Salt and pepper to taste

Steps for preparation

1. In a mug, combine the juice of half a lemon with olive oil, minced garlic, and some red pepper flakes to form a marinade.

2. Place the chicken pieces on a plain surface and create an indentation down the middle in order to increase the surface area of each chicken breast. Then, put

them in a shallow bowl, pour some olive over the chicken, and add the marinade mixture. Allow them to marinate for at least 25 minutes.

3. Mix the heavy cream, mayonnaise, mustard, and lemon juice in a small bowl to make the dressing. Mix it well and set aside.

4. Preheat your outdoor grill. Brush a bit of oil on it and put it about 4 inches away from the heat source.

5. Place the chicken on the grill, discarding any extra marinade. Grill it until the meat is cooked through, which should take roughly 4 to 5 minutes on one side. Remove it from the grill and let it cool. Slice the chicken into smaller pieces and put it in a big dish.

6. Add the apples, celery, grapes, tarragon, and dill to the chicken. Stir in the mayonnaise dressing and mix until all the ingredients are coated with the dressing. Season with some pepper and salt. Serve immediately or leave it to marinate longer overnight.

8. Grilled Lemon Chicken and Leeks

Preparation Time: 20 min | Serving: 4 | Difficulty Level: Easy

Nutritional Info: Fat: 11g | Carbs: 15g | Protein: 28g

Ingredients

- 1 tbsp. lemon zest

- 2 tbsp. fresh lemon juice

- 2 tsp. chopped rosemary

- ½ tsp. kosher salt

- ¼ tsp. black pepper

- 2 tbsp. olive oil

- 4 4-oz. chicken breasts

- 4 large leeks

- 1 tbsp. unsalted butter, cubed

- 2 garlic cloves, sliced

- 1 lemon, halved

Steps for preparation

1. Preheat your grill to about 450°F. Combine the lemon zest, salt, black pepper, lemon juice, rosemary, and 1 tablespoon of oil in a big zip-lock bag. Then, add the chicken pieces to the mixture and seal the bag. Flip the bag to coat the chicken with the marinade. Place it aside.

2. Rub half a tablespoon of oil on the leeks. Then, position the leeks over the grill and cook uncovered until grill marks appear, which should take about 7 to 8 minutes. Move the leeks to a large sheet of aluminum foil. Then, add butter and grated garlic in the foil and fold it securely.

3. Then, temporarily remove the foil from the grill and put the chicken and lemon pieces inside it, returning it to the grill. Cook the chicken fully, grilling for 2 to 4 minutes per side. Then, use some lemon juice and serve hot.

9. Chicken Pesto Kebabs

Preparation Time: 30 min | Serving: 6 | Difficulty Level: Easy

Nutritional Info: Fat: 21.3g | Carbs: 6.2g | Protein: 35g

Ingredients

- 1 cup pesto

- 1 ½ lbs. of boneless, chicken breasts pieces, cubed

- 2 pints of cherry tomatoes

- Kosher salt and black pepper (to taste)

- 2 tbsp. of chopped parsley leaves

Steps for preparation

1. In a large-sized Ziploc bag, mix the chicken with pesto, marinating it for at least 35 minutes or overnight. Drain any excess marinade and take the chicken out of the bag.

2. Thread the chicken and the cherry tomatoes onto the skewers, then season with salt and black pepper.

3. Preheat your grill until it reaches a medium-high temperature.

4. Put the skewers over the grill and flip the sides periodically until the chicken pieces are fully cooked, which should take around 12 to 15 minutes.

5. Serve hot.

10. Grilled Chicken with Balsamic Vinegar

Preparation Time: 15 min | Serving: 4 | Difficulty Level: Easy

Nutritional Info: Fat: 24g | Carbs: 7g | Protein: 42g

Ingredients

- 6 tbsp. balsamic vinegar

- 6 6-oz. skinless chicken breasts

- 2 tbsp. olive oil

- 1 garlic clove, minced

- Black pepper and salt, to taste

- 8 oz. of fresh mozzarella

- 2 large Roma tomatoes, sliced

- ¼ cup chopped basil

Steps for preparation

1. In a medium-sized saucepan, heat the balsamic vinegar over a low flame. Bring it to a boil, then decrease the heat gradually and allow it to simmer. Keep stirring

regularly until the quantity has reduced to half, which should take around 12 minutes. Now, remove it from the heat and put it aside.

2. Brush the grill gently with some oil and pre-heat it until it reaches medium-high heat. In a cup, mix the olive oil with garlic.

3. Brush some oil on both sides of the chicken, further seasoning with black pepper and salt on each side.

4. Put the chicken over a grill and cover each chicken piece with slices of mozzarella and 2 or 3 slices of Roma tomatoes. Transfer to a plate and cover with aluminum foil, allowing it to rest for 7 to 10 minutes.

5. Remove the foil and brush the tops with some basil and balsamic vinegar. Finally, sprinkle some pepper on top and serve immediately.

11. Grilled Green Chicken

Preparation Time: 10 min | Serving: 4 | Difficulty Level: Easy

Nutritional Info: Fat: 13.2g | Carbs: 20.2g | Protein: 25.4g

Ingredients

- 1 medium-sized onion

- 1 packed cup cilantro leaves

- 1 ¼ cups packed basil leaves

- ¼ cup packed mint leaves

- ¼ cup boat fish sauce

- 3 garlic cloves

- Zest of 1 lemon

- Black pepper, to taste

- 1 tsp. Aleppo pepper

- 2 tbsp. of apple juice

- ¼ tbsp. of kosher salt

- 3 lbs. of chicken thighs

- 3 limes

Steps for preparation

1. Put the onions, coriander, basil, mint leaves, fish sauce, garlic cloves, lime zest, black pepper, apple juice, and Aleppo pepper in a high-speed blender and blend the mixture until smooth.

2. Then, add some salt. This will become the marinade.

3. Put your chicken in a sealable plastic bag and add the marinade to it before refrigerating it for 8 to 12 hours. Take the bag out of the refrigerator about an hour before grilling.

4. Set your grill to a high temperature and place the chicken pieces on the grill. Now, reduce the heat to properly cook the meat from inside.

5. Grill it for about 20 minutes (or until the inside temperature is 170°F), turning every 5 to 7 minutes.

6. Serve your chicken pieces with lime slices.

12. Grilled Lime Chicken with Caesar Salad

Preparation Time: 45 min | Serving: 5 | Difficulty Level: Medium

Nutritional Info: Fat: 10.6g | Carbs: 14.1g | Protein: 25.6g

Ingredients

- 4 chicken breasts, halved

- ½ cup mesquite-lime marinade

- ½ head of lettuce, cut into small pieces

- 1 large tomato, cut into wedges

- ½ sweet onion, sliced

- 1 green bell pepper

- 2 tbsp. grated parmesan cheese

- 1 cup garlic croutons and cheese

- ½ cup creamy, Caesar-style salad dressing

Steps for preparation

1. Put the chicken pieces in a shallow pot and add the mesquite-lime marinade. Coat the pieces thoroughly, cover the top, and put it in the fridge. Allow it to marinate for about 30 minutes before cooking.

2. Preheat your coal or gas grill.

3. Proceed to grill the chicken pieces from every side for around 12 minutes. Then, remove the pieces from the heat and tear them into strips.

4. In a large container, combine the spinach, peppers, onion, cheese, croutons, dressing, and chicken. Toss the mixture until the dressing coats all the contents. Serve it hot.

13. Grilled Chicken Thighs with Jerk Sauce

Preparation Time: 30 min | Serving: 4 | Difficulty Level: Easy

Nutritional Info: Fat: 13.1g | Carbs: 9.9g | Protein: 24.7g

Ingredients

- 2 trimmed and chopped scallions

- 2 jalapeño peppers

- 2 chopped garlic cloves

- 1 tbsp. fresh thyme leaves

- 2 tbsp. of brown sugar

- 2 tbsp. lime juice

- 1 tbsp. canola oil

- 1 tbsp. soy sauce

- 1 tbsp. white vinegar

- 1½ tsp. minced ginger

- 1 tsp. ground allspice

- ½ tsp. ground nutmeg

- ¼ tsp. salt

Steps for preparation

For preparing sauce:

1. Put some scallions and jalapeños in a food processor. Proceed to pulse the contents for 5 seconds. Then, add lime juice, sauce, vinegar, garlic, sugar, and thyme, pulsing again for 10 seconds before adding the oil, ginger, nutmeg, and salt. Proceed to blend until the mixture is smooth. Place it inside a glass jar and refrigerate for later use.

To prepare chicken:

2. Place the chicken in a small bowl. Add the sauce on top and mix so that the meat is properly coated. Then, refrigerate the mixture for 6 hours.

3. Preheat the grill until it reaches medium-high heat. Take out the stored sauce and allow it to warm until it reaches room temperature.

4. Take the chicken out of the marinade.

5. Now, grill the chicken until it's tender and the thermometer, when inserted into a chicken, reads 170°F. Allow it to cool before serving. Enjoy the meal!

14. Korean Chicken Kebabs

Preparation Time: 60 min | Serving: 4 | Difficulty Level: Medium

Nutritional Info: Fat: 21.3g | Carbs: 19.2g | Protein: 14.3g

Ingredients

- ¼ cup Korean red-pepper paste

- ¼ cup reduced sodium soy sauce

- 2 tbsp. rice-wine vinegar

- 2 tbsp. light brown sugar

- 1 tbsp. toasted sesame oil

- 1 tbsp. freshly grated ginger

- 3 cloves of garlic, minced

- 2 lbs. of boneless and skinless chicken breasts

- 1½ tbsp. canola oil

- 1 large green onion, thinly sliced

- ½ tsp. toasted sesame seeds

Steps for preparation

1. In a medium-sized bowl, add soy sauce, gochujang, rice vinegar, sesame oil, brown sugar, garlic, and ginger. Mix it together and save it for later.

2. Then, take a gallon-sized Ziploc bag, add the gochujang mixture and the chicken, and let it marinate for almost 2 hours, turning the bag over occasionally. Take the chicken pieces out of the marinade and discard the rest of the marinade.

3. Preheat the grill until it is very hot. Then, thread the chicken pieces onto a few skewers, further spraying the pieces with canola oil.

4. Place the skewers on the grill and cook for almost 10 minutes, occasionally rotating the grill until the chicken pieces are fully cooked. Brush the skewers with the stored gochujang mixture and cook the chicken pieces for another 1 to 2 minutes.

5. Garnish with some green onions and sesame seeds. Serve immediately.

---

15. Grilled Chicken and Maple Rosemary Sauce

Preparation Time: 45 min | Serving: 4 | Difficulty Level: Easy

Nutritional Info: Fat: 9.1g | Carbs: 20.3g | Protein: 15.3g

Ingredients

- ½ cup maple syrup

- ¼ cup soy sauce

- 3 tbsp. olive oil

- 1 shallot, minced

- 2 tbsp. chopped rosemary

- 1 tbsp. squeezed lemon juice

- 1 tbsp. Dijon mustard

- 3 cloves of garlic, minced

- Black pepper and kosher salt, to taste

- 6 chicken breast pieces

- 2 sprigs of fresh rosemary

Steps for preparation

1. In a medium-sized bowl, mix soy sauce, maple-syrup, 2 tablespoons of olive oil, rosemary, shallots, lemon juice, garlic, and Dijon mustard together. Salt and pepper to taste.

2. In a gallon-sized Ziploc bag, add the mixture and the chicken. Leave them to marinate for almost 30 minutes, turning the bag over occasionally. Take the chicken pieces out of the bag and discard the rest of the marinade.

3. Preheat the grill so that it is hot.

4. Brush the chicken pieces with the remaining tablespoon of olive oil, further sprinkling some salt and pepper on top of them. Place the chicken pieces on the grill and cook, rotating periodically every 10 minutes until the chicken is fully cooked (reaching an internal temperature of about 165° F).

5. Serve by garnishing with rosemary, if desired.

16. Grilled Chicken Breast with Chipotle

Preparation Time: 10 min | Serving: 4 | Difficulty Level: Easy

Nutritional Info: Fat: 14g | Carbs: 9.8g | Protein: 25.5g

Ingredients

- Chipotle peppers and 1 7-oz. adobo sauce

- 1 small onion, chopped

- 2 garlic cloves

- 3 tbsp. olive oil

- 2 juiced limes

- 1 tsp. ground cumin

- 1 tsp. Mexican oregano

- 1 tsp. salt

- 1/8 cup water

- 2 chicken breast halves, butterflied

- 1 bunch of chopped fresh cilantro

Steps for preparation

1. Within your food processor, place 1 to 5 chipotle peppers with sauce, garlic, olive oil, lime juice, onion, cumin, oregano, and salt. Blend it until it becomes smooth, adding some additional water if it becomes too dense. Save a small quantity of the marinade to be used later.

2. In a resealable plastic bag, mix the chicken and marinade. Put it in the freezer for approximately 30 minutes to an hour.

3. Preheat the grill and brush some oil onto it. Then, remove the chicken from the marinade and place on the grill.

4. Grill at medium-high heat and cook well until the center is no longer pink. Cook the chicken on each side, for about 8 minutes.

5. Remove the chicken pieces from the grill and place them on the dish. Squeeze the remaining lime juice over the chicken pieces. Use cilantro as a garnish and serve.

17. Easy Home-made Grilled Chicken Fajitas

Preparation Time: 15 min | Serving: 10 | Difficulty Level: Medium

Nutritional Info: Fat: 14.1g | Carbs: 5.9g | Protein: 27g

Ingredients

- ½ cup vegetable oil

- 2 tbsp. chili powder

- 2 tbsp. lime juice

- 2 tbsp. honey

- 2 tbsp. garlic powder

- ½ tsp. paprika

- ½ tsp. black pepper

- 3 lbs. of chicken breasts

Steps for preparation

1. In a bowl, mix vegetable oil, chili powder, honey, lime juice, garlic powder, paprika, and black pepper. Then, take a large plastic bag and put the strips of chicken in it. Proceed to pour the marinade over the chicken and leave it to marinate after removing any excess air from the bag. Seal and freeze it for about 4 hours. Then, take out and defrost the meat.

2. Preheat your outdoor grill until it reaches a medium to high heat temperature. Gently brush some oil on the grate.

3. Then, take the chicken wings out of the bag and set the remaining marinade aside.

4. Cook the chicken pieces until they become slightly charred and the internal temperature of the chicken reaches 160°F (70°C).

5. Allow it to cool for five minutes. Serve immediately.

18. Michelle's Chicken Yakitori

Preparation Time: 25 min | Serving: 4 | Difficulty Level: Easy

Nutritional Info: Fat: 4.1g | Carbs: 8.4g | Protein: 37.8g

Ingredients

- ½ cup soy sauce

- ½ cup Japanese rice wine

- 1 tbsp. white sugar

- 1 tbsp. chopped ginger

- 1 ½ lb. of chicken breasts, cubed

- 4 green onion sprigs

- 8 6-inch wooden skewers

Steps for preparation

1. In a medium-sized bowl, mix the soy sauce with sugar, sake, and some ginger. Put the chicken cubes in the mixture to marinate and leave it in the freezer for 2 to 3 hours.

2. Thread the chicken pieces and green onions onto the skewers.

3. Place the marinade in a saucepan over medium-high heat and bring to a boil. Lower the temperature and allow it to simmer so that the marinade stays warm.

4. Preheat your outdoor grill and gently brush the grill with some oil. Then, add the chicken skewers and allow them to brown, for around 3 minutes on each side. When turning, brush the chicken with some of the leftover marinade so that the meat remains juicy and tender.

19. Grilled Asian Chicken

Preparation Time: 15 min | Serving: 4 | Difficulty Level: Easy

Nutritional Info: Fat: 7.6g | Carbs: 10.6g | Protein: 25.7g

Ingredients

- ¼ cup soy sauce

- 4 tsp. sesame oil

- 2 tbsp. honey

- 3 slices of fresh ginger

- 2 cloves of garlic, crushed

- 4 boneless chicken breasts

Steps for preparation

1. In a shallow microwave-safe dish, mix the soy sauce, oil, honey, ginger, and garlic. Heat it in the microwave for about 1 minute and mix the contents again. Then, heat it again for another 30 seconds, while being careful to ensure it doesn't boil.

2. Place the chicken pieces in a shallow bowl and pour the soy sauce mixture over it. Allow it to marinate for about 15 minutes.

3. Preheat the grill and brush some oil on it. Cook each side of the chicken for about 6 to 8 minutes, further basting the meat with the remaining mixture.

4. Serve immediately.

Chapter 2: Grilled Turkey Recipes

1. Teriyaki Burgers with Grilled Pineapple

Preparation Time: 10 min | Serving: 4 | Difficulty Level: Easy

Nutritional Info: Fat: 7g | Carbs: 25g | Protein: 23g

Ingredients

For the burgers:

- 1 lb. of ground turkey

- ¼ cup breadcrumbs

- 1 tbsp. fresh garlic, minced

- 1 tbsp. fresh ginger, minced

- ½ tsp. black pepper

- ¼ cup chopped fresh cilantro

- 4 rings of canned pineapple

- 1 red onion

- Hamburger buns (serving)

For the teriyaki sauce:

- ¼ cup leftover pineapple juice

- ½ cup soy sauce

- 2 tbsp. rice vinegar

- 1 tbsp. honey

- 1 tsp. minced garlic

- 2 tsp. minced fresh ginger

- 1 tbsp. cornstarch

Steps for preparation

1. Place a small saucepan on the stove and place it on a medium-high flame. Combine all the ingredients for the teriyaki sauce with the exception of the corn starch and bring the mixture to a boil. Remove the lid and cook it for about 1 minute, stirring constantly. In a separate small bowl, whisk the cornstarch and one tablespoon of water. Add the slurry, stir it, and keep the pan on the heat for an additional minute before removing.

2. In a large bowl, combine all the ingredients for the burgers and three tablespoons of teriyaki sauce. Then, mix everything well until it is combined. Then, shape the meat into thick patties and place in the refrigerator for about 30 minutes.

3. Preheat the grill to medium-high heat and lightly brush it with oil. Then, grill the pineapple rings and slices of red onion until they are caramelized and tender, which should take about 3 minutes per side. Proceed to grill the burgers. After flipping each patty, brush the meat with the sauce. Continue cooking until the burgers are cooked.

4. Place the burgers inside the buns, brush with sauce, and top with the grilled pineapple and red onion.

2. Grilled Chile-Cilantro-Lime Turkey

Preparation Time: 10 min | Serving: 4 | Difficulty Level: Easy

Nutritional Info: Fat: 9.7g | Carbs: 5.2g | Protein: 24g

Ingredients

- ¼ cup fresh lime juice

- 2 tbsp. olive oil

- 2 cloves of minced garlic

- 1 tbsp. lime zest

- 1 tsp. salt

- 1 tsp. brown sugar

- 1 tsp. red pepper flakes

- ½ tsp. ground cumin

- 4 medium-sized pieces of turkey

- 2 tbsp. chopped cilantro

Steps for preparation

1. Mix the lime juice, olive oil, garlic, and lime zest in a large bowl. Then, whisk in the cinnamon, brown sugar, red pepper flakes, and cumin. Proceed to put the turkey pieces in a wide dish and add the lime marinade.

2. Cover the bowl properly and place it in the freezer to marinate for about 30 minutes.

3. Preheat the outdoor grill until it is hot and gently brush it with some oil.

4. Put the turkey pieces on the grill and cook each side for around 5 minutes until the center is no longer pink and the meat is golden and slightly charred. Place the turkey pieces on a plate and let them rest for about 5 minutes. Lastly, slice and serve the meat with cilantro.

Chapter 3: Grilled Beef and Lamb Recipes

1. Skirt Steak Tacos

Preparation Time: 20 min | Serving: 4 | Difficulty Level: Easy

Nutritional Info: Fat: 19g | Carbs: 34g | Protein: 25g

Ingredients

- 1 lb. of skirt steak

- 1 tsp. salt

- ½ tsp. black pepper

- ½ tsp. ground cumin

- 2 tbsp. grated red onion

- 1 tsp. lime zest

- Grapeseed oil

- ¾ cup diced tomatoes

- ¼ cup thinly sliced radishes

- 1 tbsp. of fresh lime juice

- 1 tbsp. olive oil

- 8 6-inch corn tortillas, warmed

- 8 sprigs of torn cilantro

- 2 oz. of crumbled queso fresco

- 8 lime wedges (serving)

Steps for preparation

1. Preheat the grill until it reaches the temperature 450°F to 550°F. Then, sprinkle the steak with salt, pepper, and cumin. Rub the steak with the onion and lime zest.

2. Then, generously apply grapeseed oil to the grill grate. Proceed to grill the steak, for approximately 3 to 4 minutes per side. Make sure to cover it with the grill lid as it cooks. Then, remove the meat from the grill and let it rest for 10 minutes before thinly slicing the meat across the grain.

3. Finally, place the tomato pieces, lime juice, radishes, and olive oil in a small bowl. Mix them together. Then, divide the steak pieces evenly between the tortillas. Then, top each with some of the tomato mixture, cilantro, and cheese.

4. Serve with lime wedges.

2. Coffee Beef Tenderloin Steaks

Preparation Time: 5 min | Serving: 4 | Difficulty Level: Easy

Nutritional Info: Fat: 6.3g | Carbs: 5.8g | Protein: 22g

Ingredients

- 1 cup strong coffee

- 1½ tbsp. dark brown sugar

- ½ tsp. salt

- ½ tsp. pepper

- ¼ tsp. ground red pepper

- 2 garlic cloves, minced

- 4 4-oz. beef tenderloin steaks, trimmed

- Cooking spray

Steps for preparation

1. Combine the first six ingredients in a large zip-top bag. Then, add the steaks and seal the bag. Marinate it in the refrigerator for around 8 hours and turn the meat occasionally.

2. Preheat the grill and apply some cooking spray to it.

3. Proceed to remove the steaks from the marinade and discard the remainder of the marinade. Then, place the steaks on the grill rack, grilling the meat for two minutes on each side until it reaches the desired doneness.

4. Finally, serve with grilled asparagus and tomatoes.

3. Grilled Steak with Caper-Herb Sauce

Preparation Time: 30 min | Serving: 4 | Difficulty Level: Easy

Nutritional Info: Fat: 13g | Carbs: 2.4g | Protein: 16.3g

Ingredients

- 1 1-lb. boneless sirloin steak

- ¼ tsp. salt

- ¼ tsp. black pepper

- Cooking spray

- 1 cup parsley leaves

- 1 cup basil leaves

- 2 tbsp. green onions

- 2 tbsp. olive oil

- 2 tbsp. chicken broth

- 1 tbsp. capers

- 1 tbsp. fresh lemon juice

- 1 garlic clove, chopped

- 1 canned anchovy fillet, chopped

Steps for preparation

1. Prepare the grill until it reaches medium-high heat. Add some cooking spray to the grill rack.

2. Then, season the steak with some salt and pepper. Place the steak on the grill rack, grilling each side for 6 minutes. Then, allow it to rest for 10 minutes.

3. Place the parsley and remaining ingredients in the food processor and pulse it until it is blended. Slice the steak diagonally and serve with the sauce.

4. To prepare the garlic bread, grill four slices of French bread for 2 minutes on both sides or until they are toasted. Then, brush each slice with olive oil and minced garlic.

4. Grilled Lamb Chops

Preparation Time: 20 min | Serving: 6 | Difficulty Level: Easy

Nutritional Info: Fat: 17g | Carbs: 1g | Protein: 20g

Ingredients

- 1/3 cup olive oil

- ½ cup fresh mint leaves

- ¼ tsp. red pepper flakes

- Sea salt

- 12 small lamb chops

- 2 cloves of garlic, smashed

Steps for preparation

1. Preheat the grill to medium-high heat. Mix the olive oil, red pepper flakes, mint, and salt in a bowl. Then, rub the garlic on the lamb chops.

2. Place a few tablespoons of mint oil in a small bowl and use it to brush on the chops.

3. Grill the chops for 3 to 4 minutes per side.

4. Transfer the meat to a platter and brush the remaining mint oil on it. Sprinkle with the mint and serve with mint oil.

5. Garlic Butter Herb Steak in Foil Packets

Preparation Time: 15 min | Serving: 4 | Difficulty Level: Easy

Nutritional Info: Fat: 33g | Carbs: 9g | Protein: 39g

Ingredients

- 1 lb. of red potatoes, cut into fourths

- 2 carrots, sliced

- 1 red bell pepper, cubed

- 1 green bell pepper, cubed

- ½ red onion, cubed

- 1 tbsp. olive oil

- Salt and pepper

- 1 ½ lb. top sirloin steak

Garlic herb butter:

- ½ cup butter room temperature

- ¼ cup freshly chopped parsley

- 4 garlic cloves, minced

- 1 tsp. fresh rosemary, chopped

- 1 tsp. fresh thyme, chopped

- ½ tsp. salt

- ¼ tsp. pepper

Steps for preparation

1. Place the carrots, bell peppers, red potatoes, and red onion pieces in a bowl. Season with salt and pepper and add olive oil.

2. Cut out 4 pieces of aluminum foil and place the vegetable mixture on the foil. Top the vegetables with the steak.

3. In a small bowl, add the butter, rosemary, parsley, garlic, thyme, salt and, pepper. Slather the mixture on top of the steak.

4. Fold the top and ends of the foil, leaving some space for the steam to gather.

5. Then, place the packets on the grill and cover. Grill them for 15 minutes and carefully open the packets. Serve immediately.

6. Grass-fed Beef Sirloin Kebab

Preparation Time: 25 min | Serving: 4 | Difficulty Level: Easy

Nutritional Info: Fat: 10.2g | Carbs: 2g | Protein: 29g

Ingredients

- ½ cup plain Greek yogurt

- 2 tbsp. fresh dill, finely chopped

- 1 tbsp. grated lemon rind

- 1 tbsp. fresh lemon juice

- 1 tsp. kosher salt

- 1 lb. sirloin steak, trimmed

- 2 tbsp. olive oil

- 1 tsp. ground coriander

- 1 tsp. black pepper

- 8 skewers

- Cooking spray

- Green onions, chopped

Steps for preparation

1. Preheat the grill to around 450° F to 550° F. In a shallow container, mix the rind, yogurt, dill, juice, and salt. Stir everything well.

2. Cut the steak into 16 strips. Then, season it the coriander, pepper, and salt. Add some oil to the meat and thread two pieces of meat onto each skewer.

3. Place the skewers on the grill grate. Grill either side for 90 seconds until the meat is partially charred. Serve the meat with yogurt sauce and garnish with onions.

7. Olive Oil Grilled Strip Steak

Preparation Time: 25 min | Serving: 4 | Difficulty Level: Easy

Nutritional Info: Fat: 13.2g | Carbs: 3g | Protein: 26g

Ingredients

- 3 tbsp. olive oil

- 2 8-oz. New York steaks

- 1 tsp. salt

- 1 tsp. black pepper

- 1 3-inch rosemary sprig

- 1 garlic clove, crushed

- Rosemary leaves

Steps for preparation

1. Heat your grill pan over medium-high heat. Brush one tablespoon of oil over the steaks, further seasoning with half a teaspoon of black pepper and salt. Now, place the rosemary sprig, ginger, and one tablespoon of oil in a dish.

2. Put the steaks on the grill, cover it with a lid, and cook for 10 minutes or until the meat is finished. Flip the steaks and brush them with oil.

3. Put the steaks on your cutting board and allow them to rest for 5 minutes. Slice the steaks across the grain and put them on a tray. Drizzle with the leftover juice of the steaks and one tablespoon of oil.

4. Season with salt and black pepper. Garnish with rosemary if desired.

8. Grilled Beef with Salad

Preparation Time: 20 min | Serving: 6 | Difficulty Level: Easy

Nutritional Info: Fat: 17g | Carbs: 7g | Protein: 21g

Ingredients

- 2 250g sirloin steaks, trimmed
- 1 2-inch piece of fresh ginger, finely grated
- 1 garlic clove, finely grated
- 2 tbsp. lime juice
- 2 tbsp. sesame oil
- 1 tbsp. soy sauce
- 3 bird's eye red chilies
- 4 gem lettuce heads
- 12 radishes, thinly sliced
- 3 carrots, peeled and sliced
- ½ a cucumber

- 3 finely sliced spring onions

- 1 large ripe avocado, sliced

- ½ tbsp. mixed sesame seeds

Steps for preparation

1. Mix the grated ginger, garlic, lime juice, olive oil, soy sauce, and chilies in a small bowl.

2. Place the steaks over the grill and cook them for about 3 minutes on each side. Cover the steaks and set them aside for 5 minutes after they're finished cooking.

3. Arrange the lettuce leaves and put the carrots, cucumber, onion, and avocado on a baking sheet. Cut the steak across the grain and place the smaller slices over the salad. Drizzle with any remaining juices or dressing. Garnish using sesame seeds or red chilies.

9. Grilled Tri-Tip

Preparation Time: 15 min | Serving: 8 | Difficulty Level: Medium

Nutritional Info: Fat: 20.9g | Carbs: 4.4g | Protein: 38.2g

Ingredients

- 4 lbs. tri-tip roast

- 4 garlic cloves

- 1/3 cup salt

- 1/3 cup black pepper

- 1/3 cup garlic salt

Steps for preparation

1. Cut a few short slits into the roast with any sharp knife. Now, stuff the slits with a few pieces of garlic.

2. Rub salt, black pepper, and garlic salt into the meat. Then, refrigerate it for 1 hour or 24 hours. Remove the garlic from the meat and allow it to rest for 25 minutes before cooking.

3. Preheat your outdoor grill until it reaches high heat.

4. Place the meat directly over the grill for around 7 to 10 minutes and cook each side (depending on the size of the steak).

5. Lower the temperature of the grill and keep the meat on it for another 20 to 30 minutes. Do not flip the sides too often. Check the doneness of the meat using a thermometer, whereby the temperature should be about 150°F.

6. Allow the meat to rest before slicing it.

Chapter 4: Grilled Seafood Recipes

1. Shrimp Tacos (Chipotle with Mango Salsa)

Preparation Time: 5 min | Serving: 6 | Difficulty Level: Medium

Nutritional Info: Fat: 5g | Carbs: 21g | Protein: 16g

Ingredients

- 8 corn tortillas

- 1 lb. raw jumbo shrimp, peeled and deveined

- 1 tsp. chili powder

- ½ tsp. salt

- ½ cup chipotle sauce

- 2 cups mango salsa

- 1/3 cup Greek yogurt

- 2 tbsp. mayonnaise

- 2 tsp. lime juice

- ½ chipotle pepper

- 2 tsp. adobe sauce

- ¼ tsp. salt

- ½ tsp. garlic, finely chopped

- ½ tsp. cumin

Steps for preparation

1. Spray both sides of the corn tortillas with a non-stick spray. Then, cook the tortillas for around 30 to 45 seconds on both sides in a large skillet over medium heat. Set it aside.

2. Pat the peeled and deveined shrimp until it is dry and toss with chili powder and salt. After the tortillas are cooked, spray the pan with a non-stick spray and add shrimp to it.

3. Cook the pieces for around 3 to 4 minutes.

4. Top the tortillas with shrimp, mango salsa, and a tablespoon of chipotle sauce.

5. Serve immediately.

2. Spicy Filet Mignon with Grilled Sweet Onion

Preparation Time: 20 min | Serving: 4 | Difficulty Level: Easy

Nutritional Info: Fat: 3.7g | Carbs: 8.4g | Protein: 24.6g

Ingredients

- Cooking spray

- 2 cups Vidalia

- 1/7 tsp. of salt

- 1 tsp. garlic powder

- ½ tsp. ground cumin

- ½ tsp. dried oregano

- ¼ tsp. salt

- ¼ tsp. of ground red pepper

- ¼ tsp. black pepper

- 4 4-oz. filet mignon

- 2 small onions, sliced

Steps for preparation

1. Heat the grill pan over medium-high heat and apply some cooking spray to it. Then, add the onion slices to the pan and season with a pinch of salt and black pepper. Sauté the onions for eight minutes, stirring occasionally. Then, remove them from the pan and keep them warm.

2. Combine the garlic powder with the remaining 5 ingredients in a small bowl and rub into both sides of the beef. Then, proceed to grill the beef in the pan for 5 minutes.

3. Serve with the onion mixture.

3. Grilled Halibut

Preparation Time: 20 min | Serving: 4 | Difficulty Level: Easy

Nutritional Info: Fat: 7.8g | Carbs: 19.5g | Protein: 37g

Ingredients

- 2 cups plum tomatoes, seeded and diced

- 1½ cups ripe mango, diced and peeled

- ½ cup diced onion

- ½ cup chopped fresh cilantro

- 2 tbsp. lime juice

- 1 tbsp. cider vinegar

- 1 tsp. sugar

- 1 tsp. salt

- 1 tsp. black pepper

- 2 garlic cloves, minced

- 4 6-oz. halibut fillets

- 1 tbsp. olive oil

Steps for preparation

1. Preheat the grill.

2. Combine the first 7 ingredients. Then, stir in half a teaspoon of salt, half a teaspoon of pepper, and garlic.

3. Brush some oil on the halibut and sprinkle with a pinch of salt and pepper. Then, grill the fish for 3 minutes.

4. Serve with the mango salsa.

4. Chimichurri Shrimp

Preparation Time: 15 min | Serving: 4 | Difficulty Level: Easy

Nutritional Info: Fat: 6.5g | Carbs: 2g | Protein: 4g

Ingredients

- 1 cup arugula leaves

- ½ cup parsley leaves

- 2 tbsp. chopped shallots

- 2 tbsp. fresh lemon juice

- 2 tbsp. olive oil

- ¼ tsp. crushed red pepper

- 1 garlic clove

- ½ tsp. kosher salt

- Cooking spray

- 2 tsp. canola oil

- 1 lb. of shrimp (peeled, deveined, and with their tails)

- ½ tsp. black pepper

Steps for preparation

1. Preheat the grill to a high temperature.

2. Place the first seven ingredients and a pinch of salt in the food processor and pulse until it is blended.

3. Apply some cooking spray on the grill rack. Next, combine the oil and shrimp in the bowl and mix well. Then, thread four shrimp pieces onto each of the six skewers. Proceed to place the skewers on the grill rack for 2 minutes or until the shrimp is done cooking. Arrange the shrimp on the platter and season with salt and pepper. Then, add the sauce.

4. Serve.

5. Italian Grilled Shrimp

Preparation Time: 15 min | Serving: 4 | Difficulty Level: Easy

Nutritional Info: Fat: 20g | Carbs: 19g | Protein: 25g

Ingredients

- 2 tbsp. honey

- 3 tbsp. olive oil

- 1 ½ lb. of raw shrimp (with tails)

- Grapeseed oil

- 2 cups loosely packed arugula

- 1¼ cups chopped heirloom tomatoes

- ½ cup kalamata olives, halved

- ½ cup sliced red onion

- 1 tbsp. red wine vinegar

- ½ tsp. salt

- ½ tsp. black pepper

- 2 tbsp. fresh oregano leaves

Steps for preparation

1. Preheat the grill until it reaches a high temperature of 450°F to 550°F. Then, whisk together the honey and olive oil in a medium-sized bowl. Proceed to add the shrimp and toss it to coat.

2. Then, brush the grill grate with grapeseed oil. Grill the shrimp and cover with the grill lid until it is done, for about 1.5 minutes per side.

3. Then, toss together the tomatoes, olives, arugula, and onion pieces in the large bowl. Add some vinegar, olive oil, shrimp, salt, and pepper. Toss the contents, transfer the mixture to a platter, and sprinkle with oregano.

4. Serve it immediately.

6. Spinach Salad with Grilled Shrimp

Preparation Time: 30 min | Serving: 4 | Difficulty Level: Easy

Nutritional Info: Fat: 5.9g | Carbs: 6.9g | Protein: 24.8g

Ingredients

Dressing:

- 2 tbsp. of rice vinegar

- 2 tbsp. fresh orange juice

- 1.5 tbsp. extra virgin olive oil

- 1 tbsp. honey

- 1 tbsp. soy sauce

- ½ tsp. fresh ginger

- ½ tsp. salt

- 1/8 tsp. crushed red pepper

Shrimp:

- 2 tsp. extra virgin olive oil

- 1 tsp. fresh ginger, peeled

- ½ tsp. ground cumin

- ¼ tsp. salt

- ¼ tsp. black pepper

- 2 garlic cloves, minced

- 2 lbs. of large shrimps, peeled and deveined.

- Cooking spray

Salad:

- 8 cups baby spinach

- 2 cups shiitake mushroom caps

- ¾ cup red onion (sliced thin)

Steps for preparation

1. Preheat the grill.

2. Combine the first eight ingredients in the large bowl and stir well. Set the bowl aside.

3. Then, combine two teaspoons of olive oil and the next six ingredients in a large bowl. Mix the ingredients well and proceed to thread about five shrimp pieces onto the skewers. Place the skewers on the grill rack, which should be coated with the cooking spray. Proceed to grill them for three minutes or until they are done.

4. Add the spinach, mushrooms, and onion slices to the vinegar mixture and toss gently. Serve with the shrimp skewers.

7. Grilled Salmon with White Bean and Arugula Salad

Preparation Time: 30 min | Serving: 4 | Difficulty Level: Easy

Nutritional Info: Fat: 15.4g | Carbs: 21g | Protein: 40g

Ingredients

- 1 tbsp. chopped capers, rinsed and drained.

- ¼ tsp. grated lemon rind

- 3 tbsp. fresh lemon juice

- 2 tbsp. olive oil

- ¾ tsp. salt

- ½ tsp. fresh garlic, minced

- 1/8 tsp. ground red pepper

- 1 can of great northern beans, rinsed and drained

- Cooking spray

- 4 6-oz. salmon fillets

- ¼ tsp. black pepper

- 4 cups loosely packed arugula

- ½ cup sliced red onion

Steps for preparation

1. In a bowl, mix the capers, oil, salt, garlic, rind, juice, and red pepper together. Then, add the beans.

2. Place the grill pan over a medium-high flame. Then, apply some oil spray to the pan and the salmon. Proceed to season it with some salt and pepper before

placing the salmon onto the pan, skin-side down. Cook the fish for about 6 minutes before flipping it over. Sauté the other side for 1 minute or until you're finished.

3. Add the arugula and onions to the bean dish. Add any leftover capers and divide the salad and fillets between four plates. Serve immediately.

8. Shrimp Skewers and Shashti with Chimichurri

Preparation Time: 25 min | Serving: 40 | Difficulty Level: Easy

Nutritional Info: Fat: 16g | Carbs: 5g | Protein: 24g

Ingredients

- 1 cup parsley leaves

- 1 cup cilantro leaves

- ¼ cup basil leaves

- 2 garlic cloves

- ½ tsp. grated lemon rind

- 2 tbsp. lemon juice

- ¼ tsp. red pepper (crushed)

- 4 tbsp. olive oil

- ¾ tsp. salt

- 1½ lbs. of large shrimp

- 16 Shashti peppers

- ¼ tsp. black pepper

- 2 tbsp. cooking spray

Steps for preparation

1. Preheat the grill until it reaches medium-high heat.

2. Blend the parsley, coriander, basil seeds, and garlic using a food processor to make a marinade. Add some lemon juice, red pepper, 3 tablespoons of olive oil, and a pinch of salt. Blend the mixture again until most of the contents have been roughly chopped.

3. Mix the shrimps with 1/8 cup of the mixture. Thread 4 shrimps onto 8 (6") skewers and thread 6 peppers onto the 2 (8") skewers. Then, drizzle one tablespoon of olive oil onto the skewers. Proceed to sprinkle some black pepper and salt onto them.

4. Place the skewers on the grill and spray them with some oil. Grill them until the shrimps are done cooking and the peppers are charred, which should take about 3 to 5 minutes per side. Brush the remainder of the herb mixture over the skewers before eating.

9. Grilled Flounder with Banana Leaves

Preparation Time: 15 min | Serving: 4 | Difficulty Level: Easy

Nutritional Info: Fat: 17g | Carbs: 6g | Protein: 22g

Ingredients

- 1/4 cup finely chopped cilantro

- 1/4 cup olive oil

- 3 tbsp. minced shallot

- 2 tbsp. fresh lime juice

- 1 small Fresno chili, seeded and finely chopped (about 2 tbsp.)

- 1 tbsp. finely chopped lemongrass (from 1 stalk)

- 1½ tsp. light brown sugar

- 1 tsp. grated peeled fresh ginger.

- 3/4 tsp. fish sauce

- 4 6-oz. skinless flounder fillets

- ¾ tsp. salt

- 2 (12-inch square or round) banana leaves or pieces of heavy-duty aluminum foil

- 4 banana leaves for serving (optional)

Steps for preparation

1. Preheat the grill to medium-high heat (about 450°F). Combine the first 6 ingredients in a medium-sized bowl.

2. Sprinkle the fillets with some salt. Then, place the banana leaves on the grill grates and place two flounder fillets onto each leaf. Then, spoon 1/4 cup of the shallot mixture onto the fillets. Grill the fish for 5 minutes.

3. Using two spatulas, carefully remove the leaves and fish from the grill. Place each fillet onto unused banana leaves.

4. Serve immediately.

10. Grilled Mushroom Beef Burgers

Preparation Time: 20 min | Serving: 4 | Difficulty Level: Easy

Nutritional Info: Fat: 19g | Carbs: 7g | Protein: 26g

Ingredients

- 4 oz. button mushrooms

- 1 lb. ground sirloin (90% lean)

- 2 tbsp. olive oil

- 1/8 tsp. black pepper

- ¾ tsp. salt

- 1/3 cup chopped cucumber

- ¼ cup plain Greek yogurt (full fat)

- 2 tbsp. roasted minced garlic

- 1 tbsp. lemon juice

- 1 tbsp. chopped parsley

- 8 large butter lettuce leaves

- 4 heirloom tomatoes

- 4 onions, sliced

Steps for preparation

1. Preheat your grill until it reaches medium-high heat. Place the mushrooms in the food processor and blend them for around 1 minute.

2. Mix the mushrooms, ground syrup, oil, pepper, and a pinch of salt in a small bowl. Carefully shape 4 patties out of the mixture and place them on a baking sheet. The sheet must be lined with parchment paper.

3. In a shallow cup, mix the cucumber, milk, garlic, lemon juice, chopped parsley, and salt together. Set this mixture aside.

4. Put the burgers over the grill and wait until they are fully cooked, which should take around 3 minutes per side.

5. Place 3 lettuce leaves on every plate. Then, cover each using a burger patty, some tomato slices, sliced red onions, and one tablespoon of the yogurt mixture. Serve and enjoy.

---

11. Grilled Mushroom Pizzas

Preparation Time: 25 min | Serving: 4 | Difficulty Level: Easy

Nutritional Info: Fat: 16.2g | Carbs: 13.9g | Protein: 20.5g

Ingredients

- 8 oz. of mixed fresh mushrooms, sliced

- 4 tbsp. olive oil

- 4 garlic cloves, minced

- ¼ sprig of fresh rosemary

- Half a pinch of salt

- Black pepper, to taste

- 2/3 cup mozzarella cheese (shredded)

- ¼ cup parmesan cheese (shredded)

- ¼ cup marinara sauce

- 2 tbsp. red wine

- Flour (to roll the dough)

- 13.8 oz. pizza crust

Steps for preparation

1. Preheat the grill until it reaches medium-high heat. In a normal-sized saucepan, place 3 tablespoons of olive oil and sauté the mushrooms over a medium-high flame until they are golden. Lower the heat and add garlic, rosemary, and a pinch of salt and pepper. Cook the food for a few more minutes until the garlic becomes golden.

2. In the meantime, mix the parmesan and mozzarella together in a small bowl.

3. Place the dough on a hard surface and split it into quarters. Brush some olive oil on each piece and place all the ingredients near the grill.

4. Put the four pieces of dough on the grill sheet and cook them for 3 minutes before flipping each using 2 spatulas.

5. Now, spread the marinara sauce over the crust and sprinkle half of the cheese over it. Then, add the mushrooms on top and the leftover cheese. Cover your grill with a lid and cook the pizzas for around 3 to 4 minutes before the cheese melts. Make sure that the crust doesn't burn.

Note: If you do not have a grill sheet, use aluminum foil.

12. Grilled Salmon with Lemon-Pepper

Preparation Time: 15 min | Serving: 4 | Difficulty Level: Easy

Nutritional Info: Fat: 12g | Carbs: 1.3g | Protein: 34g

Ingredients

- 4 6-oz. salmon fillets (skin-on)

- 2 tbsp. unsalted butter

- 1 tsp. lemon pepper

- ½ tsp. salt

- 8 thin slices of lemon

- 4 sprigs of flat-leaf parsley

Steps for preparation

1. Preheat the grill to medium-high heat.

2. Position 4 (12") aluminum foil square pieces in a row and apply some cooking spray to each layer. Place 1 piece of salmon on each sheet, skin-side down.

3. Cover each filet with half a teaspoon of butter, one-eighth of a teaspoon of lemon pepper, a pinch of salt, 2 slices of lemon, and 1 sprig of parsley.

4. Fold the sides of every foil pack together to secure them. Place these packets on the grill and cook them for 10 to 12 minutes until they are fully cooked.

13. Grilled Red Snapper

Preparation Time: 15 min | Serving: 4 | Difficulty Level: Easy

Nutritional Info: Fat: 0.9g | Carbs: 2.8g | Protein: 29.6g

Ingredients

- 1 tbsp. smoked paprika

- 1 tsp. ground pepper

- 1 tsp. onion powder

- 1 tsp. garlic powder

- 1 tsp. dried oregano

- 1 tsp. dried thyme

- ½ tsp. salt

- ½ tsp. cayenne pepper

- 4 5-oz. red snapper fillets

- 1 tbsp. olive oil

- 4 lemon wedges

Steps for preparation

1. Preheat your grill until it is quite hot. In a small bowl, add and mix black pepper, garlic, onion powder, oregano, salt, thyme, and cayenne pepper.

2. Apply some oil to the fish and add some seasoning to each side of the fish.

3. Brush some oil on the grill rack. Now, grill the coated fish until the internal temperature reads 145°. This should take 3 to 5 minutes per side.

4. Remove the fish from the grill. Serve with lemon wedges.

14. Blackened Shrimp Tacos

Preparation Time: 20 min | Serving: 4 | Difficulty Level: Easy

Nutritional Info: Fat: 9.3g | Carbs: 30.4g | Protein: 24g

Ingredients

- 1 ripe avocado

- 1 tbsp. lime juice

- 1 small garlic clove, grated

- ¼ tsp. salt

- 1 lb. of large raw shrimps (16 to 20 pieces)

- 2 tbsp. Cajun spice (salt-free)

- 8 corn tortillas, warmed

- 2 cups chopped iceberg lettuce

- ½ cup fresh cilantro leaves

- ½ cup pico de gallo

Steps for preparation

1. Preheat the grill until it reaches medium-high heat.

2. In a shallow bowl, mash the avocados using a fork. Add some lime juice, garlic, and salt. Mix everything together.

3. Clean the shrimp and pat it dry. In a medium-sized bowl, add Cajun seasoning to the shrimps. Then, thread 5 shrimps onto 12- to 14-inch-long metal skewers. Finally, grill and flip once until the shrimps are perfectly cooked.

4. Serve the shrimps with tortillas, which should be garnished with guacamole, spinach, and cilantro. As an alternative to the guacamole, you may use Pico de Gallo.

15. Shrimp Kebabs

Preparation Time: 20 min | Serving: 6 | Difficulty Level: Medium

Nutritional Info: Fat: 14.8g | Carbs: 30.4g | Protein: 28g

Ingredients

- ¼ cup unsalted butter

- 3 cloves of garlic, minced

- 1 tbsp. Cajun seasoning

- 1 tbsp. chopped thyme

- 1 lb. of Dutch yellow potatoes

- 3 ears of corn

- 1 lb. of deveined medium-sized shrimp

- 1 12.8-oz. smoked and packaged sausage

- 2 cut lemons

- 2 tbsp. chopped parsley leaves

Steps for preparation

1. In a small bowl, mix some butter, Cajun seasoning, garlic, and thyme. Set aside.

2. Place a pot of water on the stove and allow it to boil. Add some salt and cook all the potatoes in it for 10 to 13 minutes. Mix in the corn 5 minutes before the cooking time and then drain.

3. Thread the shrimp, corn, potatoes, and sausage onto the skewers.

4. Preheat the grill until it reaches medium-high heat. Place aluminum foil on the grill.

5. Then, place the kebabs on the grill and brush them with the butter mixture. Flip the skewers halfway until the shrimp becomes opaque and the corn softens.

6. Serve the kebabs with lemon wedges and parsley, if needed.

16. Charbroiled Salmon

Preparation Time: 5 min | Serving: 4 | Difficulty Level: Easy

Nutritional Info: Fat: 24.9g | Carbs:8.6g | Protein:50.2g

Ingredients

- 1 cup soy sauce

- 2 tbsp. red wine

- ½ tsp of ground ginger

- ½ tsp. black pepper

- 2 lbs. salmon steaks

- 4 sprigs of parsley

- 4 slices of lemon

Steps for preparation

1. In a wide and sealable plastic bag, add soy sauce, red wine, ginger, salt, and black pepper. Shake the bag to mix everything together. Then, proceed to pour it over the salmon, removing any air and further sealing the bag. Refrigerate it for about 2 hours.

2. Preheat the outdoor grill to medium-high heat.

3. Cook the salmon on the hot grill for about 5 minutes on each side, further rubbing any extra marinade over it while cooking.

4. When fully cooked, garnish with parsley and serve with some lemon slices.

Chapter 5: Grilled Vegetable and Fruit Recipes

1. Grilled Artichokes

Preparation Time: 15 min | Serving: 3 | Difficulty Level: Easy

Nutritional Info: Fat: 2g | Carbs: 3g | Protein: 3.2g

Ingredients

- 3 cloves of garlic

- 2 artichokes

- 2 tsp. lemon juice

- ½ cup mayonnaise

- ½ tsp. salt

Steps for preparation

1. Slice the artichokes from the top. Proceed to trim the stems and little thorns. Slice the artichoke in half.

2. In a large pot, add enough water to cover the bottom of the pot. Then, add a bit of lemon juice and garlic to the water. Bring it to a boil and add the steamer basket to

the pot. Place the artichokes in the steamer basket, cover it, lower the heat, and then allow the water to simmer for around 20 to 30 minutes.

3. Mince one clove of garlic and mix it with lemon juice, mayonnaise, and salt. Set the mixture aside.

4. Use a spoon and scrape out the choke of the artichoke (the hair-like pointy fibers). Place the artichokes on a preheated grill and cook them for about 5 to 10 minutes, turning them frequently.

5. Serve immediately with a dipping sauce and enjoy.

2. Grilled Vegetables

Preparation Time: 10 min | Serving: 4 | Difficulty Level: Easy

Nutritional Info: Fat: 8g | Carbs: 7g | Protein: 3g

Ingredients

- 2 lbs. of assorted vegetables, halved
- 5 tbsp. olive oil
- 2 tbsp. lemon juice
- 1 tsp. salt
- 1/4 tsp. pepper
- 1½ dried Italian seasoning
- 1½ tsp. minced garlic
- ¼ cup parsley leaves, chopped
- Lemon wedges, optional

Steps for preparation

1. Combine the lemon juice, olive oil, salt, pepper, seasoning, and minced garlic in a large bowl. Then, whisk everything together.

2. Add the vegetables to the bowl and mix them until they are coated with the vinaigrette. Cover and refrigerate the bowl for 20 minutes or 2 hours.

3. Preheat the grill to medium-high heat.

4. Add denser vegetables, such as carrots. Cook them for 3 to 4 minutes and then add the rest of the vegetables to the grill.

5. Cook the vegetables for around 3 to 5 minutes per side.

6. Place the vegetables on the serving plate. Then, sprinkle with the parsley and garnish with the lemon wedges.

3. Grilled Pineapple

Preparation Time: 25 min | Serving: 4 | Difficulty Level: Easy

Nutritional Info: Fat: 3g | Carbs: 12g | Protein: 0.3g

Ingredients

- 2 tbsp. honey
- 1 tsp. olive oil
- 1 tbsp. fresh lime juice
- 1 tsp of ground cinnamon
- 8 pineapples, sliced into ½-inch thick pieces

Steps for preparation

1. In a small bowl, whisk together the honey, lime juice, olive oil, and cinnamon. Set the bowl aside.

2. Heat a grill pan and coat it with cooking spray.

3. Brush some of the marinade onto the pineapple.

4. Grill the pineapple until it is tender and golden, for about 3 to 4 minutes on each side.

5. Serve warm.

4. Pasta and Grilled Vegetables with Goat Cheese

Preparation Time: 20 min | Serving: 4 | Difficulty Level: Easy

Nutritional Info: Fat: 5.5g | Carbs: 56.3g | Protein: 14g

Ingredients

- 1 large zucchini

- 1 red bell pepper

- 1 leek, trimmed and halved

- 1 can of artichoke hearts

- 1 radicchio, quartered

- ½ tsp of salt

- ¼ tsp. black pepper

- 2 garlic cloves, minced

- Cooking spray

- 4 cups cooked Rotini

- 1 cup grape/cherry tomatoes

- ¾ cup crumbled goat cheese

- 2 tbsp. chopped fresh basil

Steps for preparation

1. Preheat the grill.

2. Place the zucchini, leek, bell pepper, artichokes, and radicchio in a single layer in a pan. Sprinkle some salt, black pepper, and garlic on top of the vegetables. Then, lightly coat the vegetables with cooking spray. Place the vegetables on the grill rack and allow them to cook for 3 minutes on all sides or until they are browned and tender. Remove the vegetables from the grill and place on a cutting board. Chop them into bite-sized pieces.

3. Place the pasta in a large bowl and season with the remaining salt. Toss well and stir in the grilled vegetables and tomatoes. Proceed to add the cheese and basil, before stirring once again.

4. Serve.

5. Grilled Okra and Tomato Skewers

Preparation Time: 25 min | Serving: 8 | Difficulty Level: Medium

Nutritional Info: Fat: 2.4g | Carbs: 5.5g | Protein: 1.3g

Ingredients

- 2 small onions, cut into 8 wedges

- 24 okra pods, trimmed

- 16 cherry tomatoes

- 4 tsp. olive oil

- 1 tsp. kosher salt

- 1 tsp. black pepper

- 1 tsp. water

- ½ tsp. ground red pepper

- 1/8 tsp. sugar

- 2 garlic cloves, minced

- Cooking spray

Steps for preparation

1. Preheat the grill.

2. Divide the onion wedges into two equal pieces. Then, thread three okra pods, two cherry tomatoes, and two onion pieces consecutively onto each of the 8 skewers.

3. Combine the olive oil, kosher salt, and remaining ingredients, with the exception of the cooking spray. Stir everything together.

4. Coat the grill rack with some cooking spray.

5. Brush the olive oil mixture onto the skewers and place them on the grill rack, cooking them for three minutes on each side or until tender.

6. Grilled Eggplant and Tomato Sandwiches with the Roquefort Dressing

Preparation Time: 15 min | Serving: 2 | Difficulty Level: Easy

Nutritional Info: Fat: 8.4g | Carbs: 42.6g | Protein: 9g

Ingredients

- ¼ cup plain yogurt

- 3 tbsp. crumbled Roquefort

- 2 tbsp. fresh parsley, minced

- 1 tbsp. light mayonnaise

- 1 garlic clove, minced

- 2 Japanese eggplants

- Cooking spray

- 8 slices of ciabatta bread

- 8 slices of tomato

- ¼ tsp of salt

- ¼ tsp. black pepper

- 2 cups trimmed arugula

Steps for preparation

1. Preheat the grill.

2. Combine the first five ingredients in the small bowl and stir everything.

3. Remove the stems of the eggplants and proceed to cut each lengthwise. Lightly coat the eggplant halves as well as the grill rack with cooking spray. Then, place the

eggplant on the rack and grill it for 3 minutes on each sides. Remove it from the grill and cut the eggplant pieces into slices. Place the bread slices on the grill rack and toast them for 3 minutes on each side.

4. Spread the yogurt mixture onto each of the four toast slices. Then, top each of them with three eggplant pieces and two tomato slices. Season with salt and pepper. Top the tomato slices with 1/2 a cup of arugula and cover with the remaining toast slices.

7. Grilled Broccoli with Lemon and Farro over Hummus

Preparation Time: 20 min | Serving: 6 | Difficulty Level: Easy

Nutritional Info: Fat: 4g | Carbs: 54g | Protein: 14g

Ingredients

- 1 cup uncooked Italian farro

- 2 lbs. of broccoli (3 large heads, cut into florets)

- 10 tbsp. olive oil

- ¼ tsp. black pepper

- 1¼ tsp. salt

- 2 quartered and seeded lemons

- 3 pieces of pita bread

- ¼ cup fresh cilantro, chopped

- ½ tsp. granulated sugar

- 1 container of hummus

Steps for preparation

1. Place a pot of water on high heat and wait for it to boil. Add the uncooked farro and lower the heat. Allow it to simmer for about 20 minutes until the farro becomes tender. Then, drain it.

2. While the farro cooks, preheat the grill until it reaches a temperature of 500°F. Apply some cooking spray to the grill. Then, mix the broccoli, oil, pepper, and salt in a large bowl.

3. Place the broccoli and lemons on the grates of the grill and keep it there until the broccoli starts to char, for around 2 to 3 minutes per side. Then, remove it from the grill.

4. Brush the pita bread with oil and toast lightly for about 1.5 minutes per side. Remove from the grill and cut into quarters.

5. Serve.

8. Grilled Pineapple Served with Toasted Coconut

Preparation Time: 20 min | Serving: 6 | Difficulty Level: Easy

Nutritional Info: Fat: 4g | Carbs: 0.9g | Protein: 2g

Ingredients

- 1/3 cup honey

- 3 tbsp. fresh lime juice

- 2 tbsp. unsalted butter, melted

- ¼ tsp. salt

- 2 3-lb. fresh pineapples, cored and quartered lengthwise

- 1 cup salted coconut chips

Steps for preparation

1. Preheat the grill to a high temperature of 500°F. Mix the honey, lime juice, butter, and salt in a small bowl.

2. Brush a quarter of the honey mixture on the pineapple pieces and let them rest for 5 minutes.

3. Apply some oil to the grill grate. Then, place the pineapple quarters on it and cover, further flipping them once the pieces are slightly charred after about 8 to 10 minutes. Transfer the pineapple to the serving platter.

4. Top with some coconut chips and drizzle with the remaining honey mixture.

9. Grilled Tofu Burgers with Lemon-Basil

Preparation Time: 20 min | Serving: 4 | Difficulty Level: Easy

Nutritional Info: Fat: 11.3g | Carbs: 34.5g | Protein: 10.5

Ingredients

- 1/3 cup chopped fresh basil
- 2 tbsp. Dijon mustard
- 2 tbsp. honey
- 2 tsp. grated lemon rind
- ¼ cup fresh lemon juice
- 1 tbsp. extra virgin olive oil
- ½ tsp. salt
- ¼ tsp. black pepper
- 4 garlic cloves, minced
- 1 lb. firm tofu, drained
- Cooking spray
- ⅓ cup kalamata olives, pitted and chopped
- 3 tbsp. sour cream
- 3 tbsp. light mayonnaise
- 6 hamburger buns
- 6 tomato slices

- 1 cup trimmed watercress

Steps for preparation

1. Place the first eight ingredients and 3 garlic cloves in a small bowl. Then, cut the tofu crosswise into six slices. Then, pat each square dry and place the tofu slices on the jelly roll pan. Then, brush both sides of the tofu slices with the lemon juice mixture and preserve the remaining juice mixture. Then, let the tofu stand for 1 hour.

2. Preheat the grill and coat it with some oil.

3. Place the tofu slices on the grill rack and grill for around 3 minutes on each side, brushing them with the leftover juice.

4. Then, in a small bowl, combine the remaining minced garlic clove, chopped olives, sour cream, and mayonnaise. Mix well and spread the mayonnaise over the bottom half of both hamburger buns. Then, add one tofu slice, tomato slice, two tablespoons of watercress, and the top half of the bun.

5. Serve and enjoy.

10. Grilled Peaches and Gingersnap Crumble

Preparation Time: 15 min | Serving: 4 | Difficulty Level: Easy

Nutritional Info: Fat: 9g | Carbs: 29g | Protein: 3g

Ingredients

- 1 tbsp. liquid cane sugar

- ½ tsp. ground cinnamon

- ½ tsp. ground ginger

- Canola oil

- 6 medium-sized fresh peaches, halved and pitted

- 1/3 cup heavy cream

- ½ tsp. vanilla extract

- 4 gingersnaps, roughly chopped

- 2 tbsp. fresh mint, sliced

Steps for preparation

1. Preheat the charcoal grill until it reaches the medium-high temperature of 400°F to 450°F. Then, mix together the cane sugar, cinnamon, and ginger in a small bowl. Brush the grill grates with some oil.

2. Place the peach halves on the grates and grill them until marks appear, which should take around 3 to 4 minutes. Flip the peaches and brush the tops with the sugar-cinnamon mixture. Continue grilling until the fruit become tender and the glaze begin to brown, which should take around 4 minutes. Remove them from the grill.

3. Beat the cream and vanilla until soft peaks form, for around 1 minute. Then, place three peach halves in four shallow bowls and mix them with the whipped cream.

4. Finally, top the mixture with the gingersnaps and mint. Serve immediately.

11. Perfect Grilled Zucchini

Preparation Time: 10 min | Serving: 4 | Difficulty Level: Easy

Nutritional Info: Fat: 3.5g | Carbs: 4g | Protein: 1g

Ingredients

- 2 medium-sized zucchini

- 1 tbsp. olive oil

- 1 tbsp. red wine vinegar

- 1 tsp. dried parsley

- 1 tsp. dried basil

- ½ tsp. garlic powder

- Kosher salt

- Black pepper

Steps for preparation

1. Preheat the grill until it reaches medium-high heat. Cut the zucchini into strips and put it in a large bowl. Then, add oil, parsley, basil, red wine vinegar, garlic powder, salt, and black pepper.

2. Place the zucchini on the grill and cook it for 2 to 3 minutes. Flip and continue cooking it on high heat while covered, for about 2 to 3 minutes. Remove from the heat.

3. Serve.

12. Grilled Garlic Broccoli

Preparation Time: 25 min | Serving: 4 | Difficulty Level: Easy

Nutritional Info: Fat: 7g | Carbs: 7g | Protein: 3g

Ingredients

- 4 cups broccoli florets
- 2 tbsp. olive oil
- ½ tsp. salt
- ½ tsp. black pepper
- ½ tsp. garlic powder
- ¼ tsp. red pepper flakes

Steps for preparation

1. Place the broccoli, salt, pepper, oil, and garlic powder in a bowl and mix, ensuring that the broccoli is seasoned well.

2. Then, place a large piece of foil on the grill. Put the broccoli on the foil and grill it for around 8 to 10 minutes until it gets slightly crisp.

3. Enjoy your broccoli!

13. Grilled Tofu with Spicy Peanut Sauce

Preparation Time: 10 min | Serving: 4 | Difficulty Level: Easy

Nutritional Info: Fat: 22g | Carbs: 12g | Protein: 14g

Ingredients

- 2 packs of tofu, drained

- Grapeseed oil

- 2 tbsp. light brown sugar

- ½ tsp. black pepper

- 1 tsp. salt

- ¼ cup of packed cilantro leaves

- 3 tbsp. salted peanuts

- 2 tbsp. olive oil

- 2 tbsp. toasted sesame oil

- 2 tbsp. rice vinegar

- 1 small garlic clove

- 1 red chili, seeded and chopped

- 2 tsp. fresh ginger, chopped

- 1 tsp. of fresh lime juice

Steps for preparation

1. Preheat the grill until it reaches around 450°F to 550°F. Then, cut the tofu in half in order to have four tofu strips. Wrap each strip in many layers of paper towels and leave them for 10 minutes.

2. Then, remove the paper towels and lightly brush the tofu with some grapeseed oil. Now, sprinkle some brown sugar, pepper, and salt over the tofu.

3. Pulse the remaining ingredients in the food processor.

4. Apply some grapeseed oil to the grill rack and grill the tofu until grill marks appear, for around 2 to 3 minutes per side. Then, cut each strip into three triangles.

5. Serve the tofu with some peanut sauce.

14. Grilled Vegetables Served with Creamy Turmeric Sauce.

Preparation Time: 25 min | Serving: 4 | Difficulty Level: Easy

Nutritional Info: Fat: 0g | Carbs: 0g | Protein: 0g

Ingredients

- 1/3 cup of whole-fat Greek yogurt

- 2 tbsp. of extra virgin olive oil

- ½ tsp. of ground turmeric

- 1 garlic clove, minced

- 2 tsp. lemon zest

- 1 tbsp. fresh lemon juice

- 1 tsp. salt

- 1 tsp. black pepper

- 1 large eggplant

- 1 large red bell pepper

- 1 large zucchini

- Grapeseed oil

- ¼ cup of pomegranate arils

- 3 tbsp. mint leaves

Steps for preparation

1. Preheat the grill to about medium-high heat (around 450°F). Mix the yogurt, turmeric, garlic, olive oil, lemon zest, lemon juice, and one tablespoon of water in a small bowl. Then, stir in some salt and black pepper.

2. Proceed to cut the eggplant lengthwise. Then, brush the bell pepper, yellow squash, zucchini, and eggplant with the grapeseed oil.

3. Now, generously apply grapeseed oil to the grill grate. Place the eggplant, zucchini, and yellow squash on the grill. Turn each piece once after around 10 minutes. Now, grill the bell pepper, while occasionally turning the pieces, for around 5 minutes.

4. Cut the eggplant diagonally into slices. Transfer the grilled vegetables to the platter and season with salt and black pepper. Finally, drizzle the sauce on the vegetables and sprinkle with pomegranate arils and mint.

5. Enjoy.

15. Grilled Tropical Fruit with Almond-Ricotta Sauce

Preparation Time: 10 min | Serving: 4 | Difficulty Level: Easy

Nutritional Info: Fat: 2g | Carbs: 1.3 | Protein: 4g

Ingredients

- ½ cup vanilla Greek yogurt

- ¼ cup of ricotta cheese

- 3 tbsp. packed brown sugar

- ¼ tsp. almond extract

- 1 fresh pineapple, peeled and cored

- 2 bananas, unpeeled

- Berries

- Coconut flakes

Steps for preparation

1. Combine the yogurt, brown sugar, ricotta cheese, and almond extract in a small bowl and stir well. Then, cover and chill in the refrigerator until it is to be served.

2. Clean the grill and spray some oil on the grates.

3. Preheat the grill until it reaches medium-high heat.

4. Lay the pineapple on the grill rack and close the lid. Turn the pineapple occasionally and wait until grill marks appear on each side, which should take about 8 to 10 minutes.

5. Place the unpeeled bananas on the grill and wait until sear marks appear.

6. Remove the fruit from the grill and serve with the almond-ricotta sauce, fresh berries, and coconut.

16. Grilled Avocado Stuffed with Chickpeas and Tahini

Preparation Time: 20 min | Serving: 4 | Difficulty Level: Easy

Nutritional Info: Fat: 14.2g | Carbs: 17.4g | Protein: 5.2g

Ingredients

- 1 can of chickpeas, drained

- Oil Spray

- ½ tsp. smoked paprika

- Salt and pepper

- 2 large avocados

- ½ cup cucumber, diced

- ½ cup cherry tomatoes

- 1½ tbsp. fresh lemon juice

- 2 tbsp. tahini

- Cilantro

Steps for preparation

1. Preheat the grill to medium-high heat.

2. Place the chickpeas in a small bowl and wait for them to dry. Then, spray them with grapeseed oil spray and add smoked paprika, salt, and pepper.

3. Place chickpeas in the bottom of the grill basket. Place on the grill and cook for around 10 minutes. Spray the chickpeas again with the grapeseed spray and stir. Then, cook for another ten minutes until they become crispy. Remove them from the heat and allow them to cool.

4. Cut the avocados in half and scoop out the seed. Spray some grapeseed oil on the avocados and season with salt and pepper. Place the fleshy-side down on the grill and allow it to grill until marks form, which should take about five minutes.

5. Mix the cucumber, tomatoes, and lemon juice in a small bowl and season with salt and pepper.

6. Divide the cucumber mixture into each of the avocado halves. Then, top each of the halves with one tablespoon of the prepared chickpeas. Drizzle with Tahini.

7. Serve and enjoy.

17. Grilled Sweet Potato Fries

Preparation Time: 5 min | Serving: 4 | Difficulty Level: Easy

Nutritional Info: Fat: 5g | Carbs: 19g | Protein: 1g

Ingredients

- 4 large sweet potatoes

- 2 tbsp. salt

- 2 tbsp. olive oil

- 1 tbsp. brown sugar

- 1 tsp. chipotle chili pepper

- French cilantro, chopped

Steps for preparation

1. Place the potatoes in a large pot of cold water. Add salt, bring to a boil, and allow the potatoes to cook until they are tender, for about 10 to 15 minutes.

2. Drain and let them cool slightly. Now, heat the grill until it reaches medium-high heat.

3. Slice the potatoes into wedges and peel off the skins. Place the wedges in a bowl and drizzle with olive oil. Season with some brown sugar, a teaspoon of salt, and chipotle chili pepper. Mix them together until the potatoes are evenly coated.

4. Grill the sweet potato fries for about 6 minutes until they become lightly golden. Remove the potatoes from the platter.

5. Serve.

18. Grilled Cauliflower Steaks

Preparation Time: 15 min | Serving: 4 | Difficulty Level: Easy

Nutritional Info: Fat: 8g | Carbs: 16g | Protein: 5g

Ingredients

- 2 large heads of cauliflower
- 2 tbsp. olive oil
- 2 lemons, zested and juiced
- 2 cloves of garlic, minced
- 1 tsp. honey
- 2 tsp. salt
- ¼ tsp. red pepper flakes
- ¼ cup of fresh parsley, chopped
- ¼ cup of toasted walnuts, chopped
- Lemon wedges

Steps for preparation

1. Remove the outer leaves of the cauliflower head. Then, remove the bottom stem end to create a flat base. Rest the cauliflower on its stem, trim away the sides, and cut the remaining head to create 2, 3, or more "steaks."

2. Keep the sides of the cauliflower. In a small bowl, combine the olive oil, lemon zest, lemon juice, garlic, and honey. Mix them together.

3. Heat the grill to a medium-high temperature. Apply the mixture to the cauliflower steak and then season with salt.

4. Place the salted side down on the hot grill and brush the tops of the steaks with olive oil. Season them with salt. Then, cover the grill and let the steaks cook for about 5 to 6 minutes.

5. Flip them and cook for an additional 5 minutes. Remove from the grill.

6. Then, garnish the steaks with red pepper flakes, walnuts, and parsley.

7. Serve hot along with lemon wedges.

---

19. Mini Pineapple Pizzas

Preparation Time: 20 min | Serving: 6 | Difficulty Level: Easy

Nutritional Info: Fat: 7.1g | Carbs: 12g | Protein: 8g

Ingredients

- 1 medium-sized pineapple, peeled and cored
- 2 tbsp. canola oil
- 8 slices of Canadian bacon
- ½ cup red onion
- 2/3 cup mozzarella cheese, shredded.
- ½ cup pizza sauce
- 2 tbsp. black olives

- 3 tbsp. fresh basil, chopped

- ½ tsp. red pepper flakes

Steps for preparation

1. Preheat the broiler until it reaches a high temperature, keeping the oven rack 6 inches away from the heat source.

2. Now, heat the grill pan over a medium-high flame. Cut the pineapple into 8 pieces and brush some oil on the individual pieces. Proceed to place the pineapple rounds over a grill pan and cook for 3 minutes on each side until sear marks appear. Transfer the pieces to a baking sheet.

3. Then, place the Canadian bacon slices over the grill pan and cook them for 1 to 2 minutes on both sides. Then, set them aside.

4. Heat the remaining oil in a separate nonstick skillet on medium-high heat. Then, add the onions and cook them for 3 to 4 minutes. Keep stirring until they soften.

5. Then, top each pineapple slice with cheese, a slice of Canadian bacon, and pizza sauce. Place some additional cheese on top, along with onions and black olives. Broil the pineapple pizzas at a high temperature for 2 to 3 minutes until the cheese melts. Sprinkle basil and red pepper flakes on top of each pizza.

6. Serve and enjoy.

20. Grilled Eggplant

Preparation Time: 15 min | Serving: 4 | Difficulty Level: Easy

Nutritional Info: Fat: 7.3g | Carbs: 8.3g | Protein: 1.4g

Ingredients

- 1 large or small eggplants

- 2 tbsp. olive oil

- ¼ tsp. salt

Steps for preparation

1. Preheat your grill to medium-high heat.

2. In a wide bowl, mix the eggplant with cooking oil. Then, sprinkle some salt and stir them again. Finally, grill the eggplant and mix until it is tender.

3. Serve immediately.

21. Parmesan with Grilled Zucchini

Preparation Time: 20 min | Serving: 4 | Difficulty Level: Easy

Nutritional Info: Protein: 6.5g | Carbss: 2.7g | Fat: 17.5g

Ingredients

- ¼ cup olive oil

- 2 garlic cloves, finely chopped

- ¼ tsp. crushed red pepper

- ½ cup panko whole-wheat breadcrumbs

- ½ cup grated Parmesan cheese

- 1½ tsp. fresh thyme leaves

- 1 tsp. lemon zest

- ¼ tsp. salt

- 2 large zucchini

- Lemon wedges (serving)

Steps for preparation

1. Place a small size skillet over a low flame. Add some oil and wait for it to heat up. Then, add some red pepper and garlic, stirring constantly until the garlic softens and becomes golden, which should take around 4 to 5 minutes.

2. Remove it from the heat and leave it to cool for 3 minutes. Stir in the panko, parmesan cheese, thyme, and lemon zest. Salt to taste.

3. Preheat the grill until it reaches a high temperature. Now, put some oil over the grill. Finally, put the zucchini on the grill and allow it to cook uncovered until it becomes tender, which should take around 4 minutes for each side.

4. Pour the panko mixture on top of the zucchini. Grill until the cheese is broiled, for about 3 to 5 minutes. Remove from the heat and serve with a lemon slice.

22. Grilled Potatoes

Preparation Time: 15 min | Serving: 4 | Difficulty Level: Easy

Nutritional Info: Fat: 6g | Carbs: 38.3g | Protein: 5g

Ingredients

- 4 russet potatoes (about 8 oz. each)

- 1 tbsp. olive oil

- ½ tsp. ground pepper

- ½ tsp. garlic powder

- ½ tsp. paprika

- ½ tsp. salt

- ¼ cup sour cream

- 2 tbsp. fresh chives, chopped

Steps for preparation

1. Preheat the grill.

2. Place each potato over a different, double-layered piece of aluminum foil. Drizzle the olive oil on the potatoes and mix to allow them to become evenly coated with the oil. Sprinkle some pepper, garlic powder, paprika, and salt on the potatoes and wrap them securely in a piece of aluminum foil.

3. Place the aluminum foil packet over the surface of the grill and leave it for around 1 hour.

4. Remove the wrapped potatoes from the grill and allow them to cool. Then, unwrap them and create a slit in every potato, further fluffing them with a fork.

5. Cover them with sour cream, chips, and a pinch of salt.

23. Pesto Butter with Grilled Corn

Preparation Time: 30 min | Serving: 4 | Difficulty Level: Easy

Nutritional Info: Fat: 9.2g | Carbs: 20.1g | Protein: 4.9g

Ingredients

- 1 tbsp. butter, softened

- ½ tsp. lemon zest

- ½ tsp. kosher salt

- ½ tsp. ground pepper

- ¼ tsp. grated garlic

- ¼ cup sliced fresh basil

- ¼ cup of parmesan cheese, grated

- 4 ears of corn

- 1 tbsp. canola oil

Steps for preparation

1. Heat the grill until it becomes very hot.

2. Use a small food processor and put inside it butter, salt, pepper, lemon zest, garlic, two tablespoons of parmesan cheese, and basil. Then, blend it together until it is smooth. Alternatively, you can mash them in a bowl by using a fork.

3. Brush some oil on the corn. Then, grill the ears of corn and rotate them periodically until they are finely roasted and soft, for about 6 to 8 minutes.

4. Finally, spread the butter mixture on top of the corn and sprinkle two teaspoons of parmesan and basil on top.

5. Serve immediately.

24. Grilled Peaches with Vanilla Mascarpone

Preparation Time: 10 min | Serving: 4 | Difficulty Level: Easy

Nutritional Info: Fat: 11g | Carbs: 14g | Protein: 2g

Ingredients

- 2 large, ripe fresh peaches

- 2 tbsp. olive oil

- 5 tsp. pure maple syrup

- 3 tbsp. vanilla whole-fat Greek yogurt

- 1 tbsp. mascarpone cheese, at room temperature

- 1 tbsp. small fresh mint leaves

Steps for preparation

1. Preheat the grill to around 450°F or place a grill pan over medium-high heat. Apply some oil to the peaches. Spray a bit of oil on the grate as well.

2. Put the peach halves on the grate, ensuring that they are placed down on the grill on the side they have been cut. Cook them uncovered for about 2 minutes or until sear marks form.

3. Flip the sides and brush one teaspoon of maple syrup on every piece. Then, grill the pieces until they are tender, which should take about 2 more minutes.

4. In a shallow bowl, mix cream, mascarpone, and one teaspoon of maple syrup. You can serve the peaches hot or at a normal temperature, such as with a combination of mascarpone and mint.

25. Grilled Avocado Salsa with Salmon and Tomato

Preparation Time: 20 min | Serving: 4 | Difficulty Level: Easy

Nutritional Info: Fat: 24g | Carbs: 9g | Protein: 38g

Ingredients

- 2 cups of cubed avocados

- 1 cup heirloom yellow cherry tomatoes

- 2 tbsp. chopped cilantro

- ½ tsp. chopped serrano chili

- 1½ tbsp. sliced shallots

- 1 tsp. fresh lime juice

- 1 tsp. salt

- ¾ tsp. black pepper

- 1 tbsp. olive oil

- 4 salmon fillets (with skins)

Steps for preparation

1. Preheat your grill until it reaches a high temperature. In a medium-sized dish, mix the avocadoes, onions, cilantro leaves, serrano, and shallots together. In a shallow cup,

whisk together some lime juice, a pinch of salt, and a bit of black pepper. Then, drizzle the juice over the avocado mixture.

2. Brush the salmon with some olive oil and sprinkle some salt and black pepper on the meat.

3. Place the salmon (skin-side) down on the grill. Cook the meat for a few minutes, flipping once until the salmon is fully cooked, around 2 minutes per side.

4. Serve hot.

26. Grilled Feta Panzanella and Tomato

Preparation Time: 20 min | Serving: 4 | Difficulty Level: Easy

Nutritional Info: Fat: 21g | Carbs: 39g | Protein: 13g

Ingredients

- 2 lbs. heirloom tomatoes

- 4 oz. halved French bread

- ¼ cup olive oil

- 1 3-oz. feta cheese

- ¼ tsp. salt

- ¼ tsp. black pepper

- 1 14.5-oz. can unsalted cannellini beans

- ½ cup sliced red onion

- ½ cup chopped basil leaves

- 2 tsp. red wine vinegar

Steps for preparation

1. Heat the grill to 450°F or 540°F. Brush the tomatoes and pieces of bread with 1 tablespoon of olive oil and place them, along with the feta cheese, over the grill.

Allow them to grill until sear marks appear, repeating this on all sides, which should take approximately 2 to 4 minutes per side.

2. Transfer the food to the plate and sprinkle some salt and black pepper on top. Allow the pieces to cool for 5 minutes, further cutting the tomatoes and bread into bite-size pieces.

3. Place the tomatoes, bread pieces, beans, onion slices, basil, vinegar, and 4 tablespoons of olive oil in a wide bowl. Mix the salad gently and divide it into 4 plates, scattering the feta uniformly over the end. Serve straight away.

27. Grilled Crunchy Coleslaw

Preparation Time: 15 min | Serving: 4 | Difficulty Level: Easy

Nutritional Info: Fat: 19.2g | Carbs: 3.6g | Protein: 27.1g

Ingredients

- ½ head of red cabbage

- 2 tbsp. canola oil

- 1 tbsp. sugar

- Pinch of salt

- Black pepper, to taste

- 1 tsp. orange zest

- 1 tsp. Dijon mustard

- 1 tbsp. fresh orange juice

- ¼ cup olive oil

- ¼ cup parsley, chopped

- 1 onion, chopped

Steps for preparation

1. Preheat the grill until it reaches medium-high heat. Put the cabbage on the baking sheet and drizzle some vegetable oil on it.

2. Sprinkle cinnamon, salt, and black pepper over the cabbage. Grill the cabbage for about 5 minutes on each side, or 10 minutes in total, flipping everything once or twice before the edges wilt in order to ensure that the cabbage stays crunchy.

3. Remove the cabbage from the grill and let it cool for a few minutes. Now, create a vinaigrette in a small-sized cup, whisking together the citrus zest, mustard, orange juice, and olive oil.

4. Add half a pinch of salt and pepper. Chop the roasted cabbage, remove the core, and place it in a bowl. Proceed to pour the dressing in, further adding some green onion and chopped parsley. Then, toss to mix well. Serve immediately.

28. Grilled Watercress Chimichurri with Halloumi

Preparation Time: 15 min | Serving: 3 | Difficulty Level: Easy

Nutritional Info: Fat: 12.9g | Carbs: 20.2g | Protein: 7.9g

Ingredients

- 1 cup fresh cilantro

- 1/3 cup fresh watercress

- 3 garlic cloves, minced

- 6 tbsp. olive oil

- 4 tbsp. red wine vinegar

- 1 red chili pepper, diced

- Pinch of salt

- 8 oz. Halloumi, sliced

- 2 tbsp. olive oil

Steps for preparation

1. Cut the watercress and cilantro into medium-sized pieces. Then, in a separate cup, mix the garlic cloves, olive oil, vinegar, chili pepper, and half pinch of salt. Proceed to place all the ingredients in a food processor.

2. Brush the grill with a bit of olive oil and heat it so that it becomes very hot. Put the halloumi slices over the grill.

3. Now, grill each slice for 4 to 5 minutes. Make sure to flip and roast the other side. Repeat this process with the remaining pieces of halloumi. If you want to keep them warm, you may move them to a tray and cover them with aluminum foil.

4. Finally, serve the slices with chimichurri.

29. Marinated Grilled Tomatoes

Preparation Time: 10 min | Serving: 6 | Difficulty Level: Easy

Nutritional Info: Fat: 0g | Carbs: 4g | Protein: 5g

Ingredients

- 1 lb. assorted tomatoes

- ¼ cup red wine vinegar

- 2 tbsp. olive oil

- 2 tbsp. shallots, chopped

- 1 tsp. garlic, finely chopped

- 1 tsp. salt

- ½ tsp. black pepper

- ¾ cup fresh basil, chopped

Steps for preparation

1. Preheat the grill until it becomes very hot. Remove the cores of the tomatoes and cut them into three slices lengthwise.

2. Put the tomatoes in a large bowl. Then, add vinegar, followed by the milk, shallots, salt, and 1/3 cup of basil. Mix well until the tomatoes are fully covered. Leave the tomatoes in place for 10 minutes.

3. Brush some oil on the grill. Then, place the tomatoes on the oiled grates. Brush the sides with the vinegar-oil mixture. Grill them until they are fully cooked, for about 3 to 5 minutes.

4. Then, flip them to cook each side for one minute. Move the tomatoes to a plate; put the remaining mixture over the tomatoes and place the remainder of the basil on top.

30. Grilled Potatoes

Preparation Time: 15 min | Serving: 4 | Difficulty Level: Easy

Nutritional Info: Fat: 6g | Carbs: 38.3g | Protein: 5g

Ingredients

- 4 russet potatoes (about 8 oz. each)

- 1 tbsp. olive oil

- ½ tsp. ground pepper

- ½ tsp. garlic powder

- ½ tsp. paprika

- ½ tsp. salt

- ¼ cup sour cream

- 2 tbsp. fresh chives, chopped

Steps for preparation

1. Preheat the grill.

2. Place each potato on a different, double-layered piece of aluminum foil. Drizzle the oil generously on the potatoes and flip them to ensure that they are coated

well. Sprinkle some pepper, garlic powder, paprika, and a pinch of salt. Wrap the potatoes securely in a piece of foil.

3. Place the potato packets on the surface of the grill and keep them there for around 1 hour, until they become tender.

4. Remove the wrapped potatoes from the grill. Let them cool and unwrap. Then, cut a slit into every potato and fluff using a fork. Cover with sour cream and chips, before adding a pinch of salt.

5. Serve immediately.

31. Grilled Packets with Caraway, Smoked Sausage, and Cabbage

Preparation Time: 20 min | Serving: 6 | Difficulty Level: Medium

Nutritional Info: Fat: 21g | Carbs: 13.1g | Protein: 8.8g

Ingredients

- ½ -inch-thick round smoked sausage

- 3 tbsp. olive oil

- 10 cups red cabbage, shredded

- 1 large onion, sliced

- 3 tbsp. red-wine vinegar

- 1 tsp. caraway seeds

- ¼ tsp. pepper

- 1/8 tsp. salt

Steps for preparation

1. Preheat the grill until it reaches medium-high heat. Cut out 6 (14-inch) aluminum foil pieces. Cover 1 side of every sheet of aluminum foil with some oil.

2. Mix the sausage and 1 tablespoon of oil in a wide bowl until the former is evenly coated. Then, proceed to separately mix together the cabbage, onion slices, vinegar, caraway seeds, sliced bell pepper, salt, and some oil in another bowl.

3. Mix everything together and divide the contents equally between the foil sheets. Now, top the vegetables on each aluminum sheet with some of the sausage.

4. Flip the longer sides of every piece of aluminum foil and fold the non-closed edges of every piece of foil to create a packet.

5. Put these packets on the grill and cook them until all the vegetables soften and become mildly charred, which should take around 20 minutes.

32. Grilled Shallot-Herb Vinaigrette with Vegetables

Preparation Time: 30 min | Serving: 8 | Difficulty Level: Easy

Nutritional Info: Fat: 9.1g | Carbs: 9.2g | Protein: 2g

Ingredients

- 8 small ripe tomatoes

- 4 whole baby eggplants

- 8 baby summer squash

- 16 mini sweet peppers

- 1 bunch trimmed scallions

- 5 tbsp. olive oil

- ¾ tsp. salt

- ½ tsp. ground pepper

- 2 tbsp. sherry vinegar

- 1 tbsp. shallot, diced

- 1 tbsp. fresh herbs, chopped

Steps for preparation

1. Preheat the grill until it reaches medium-high heat.

2. In a large bowl, mix the tomatoes, eggplant, squash, peppers, and scallions. Proceed to add 3 tablespoons of oil and half a teaspoon of salt and pepper each to the vegetables.

3. Brush the oil over the grill rack. Then, grill all the vegetables, regularly flipping them, until they have become soft and slightly charred, which should take around 6 minutes. Move them to the serving plate.

4. Mix together the vinegar, shallots, herbs, 2 tablespoons of olive oil, and a pinch of salt in a medium-size bowl. Drizzle the mixture over the grilled vegetables.

5. Serve hot.

33. Grilled Carrots

Preparation Time: 5 min | Serving: 4 | Difficulty Level: Easy

Nutritional Info: Fat: 3.8g | Carbs: 12.7g | Protein: 12g

Ingredients

- 1½ lb. large carrots

- 1 tbsp. olive oil

- ½ tsp. salt

- 1 tbsp. cilantro, chopped

- ½ tbsp. lime

- ¼ tsp. cumin

- ¼ tsp. black pepper

Steps for preparation

1. Preheat the grill until it reaches medium-high heat.

2. Peel the carrots and break them into pieces.

3. Place the carrots in a small bowl and drizzle some extra virgin olive oil on them. Add some salt to them.

4. Place the carrots over the grill and cook them for about 8 to 10 minutes, rotating them regularly.

5. Roughly chop the cilantro and pour in a bowl. Add the carrots, the juice of half a lime, cumin, and some salt. Mix and serve immediately.

34. Grilled Garlic and Herb Zucchini

Preparation Time: 15 min | Serving: 4 | Difficulty Level: Easy

Nutritional Info: Fat: 15g | Carbs: 19.2g | Protein: 25.3g

Ingredients

- 4 tbsp. olive oil

- ¼ cup shallot, minced

- 2 cloves garlic, minced

- 2 tbsp. rosemary, chopped

- 2 tbsp. parsley leaves, chopped

- Salt and ground black pepper, to taste

- 2 medium-sized zucchini

- 1 medium-sized yellow squash, sliced

Steps for preparation

1. Preheat the grill until it is very hot.

2. In a medium-sized bowl, mix 3 tablespoons of olive oil with the garlic, shallot, parsley, and rosemary. Season with salt and pepper before setting aside.

3. Brush the squash and zucchini with the remaining tablespoon of olive oil, further seasoning with some salt and pepper.

4. Place some vegetables on the grill and cook them until they soften, for almost 2 minutes on each side.

5. Serve with the olive oil mixture.

Chapter 6: Grilled Salad Recipes

1. Grilled Snapper with Orzo Pasta Salad

Preparation Time: 20 min | Serving: 4 | Difficulty Level: Easy

Nutritional Info: Fat: 11.2g | Carbs: 39.3g | Protein: 32.7g

Ingredients

- 1½ cups uncooked orzo

- Cooking spray

- 4 6-oz. red snapper fillets

- ½ tsp. salt

- ¼ tsp. black pepper

- 1½ tbsp. shallots, minced

- 1 tbsp. fresh parsley, chopped

- 1 tbsp. fresh lemon juice

- 2 tsp. orange juice

- 1 tsp. Dijon mustard

- 2½ tbsp. extra virgin olive oil

Steps for preparation

1. Boil the pasta without any salt. Drain and keep warm.

2. Heat the grill pan over medium-high heat and coat it with cooking spray. Season the fish with salt and pepper and sauté it in the pan. Cook it for 3 minutes on both sides.

3. Combine the remaining salt, pepper, shallots, parsley, orange juice, lemon juice, and mustard in a small bowl. Stir well and slowly add the olive oil, while constantly stirring with the whisk. Drizzle the shallot mixture over the pasta and toss well until the pasta is evenly coated.

4. Serve immediately.

2. Grilled Romaine Salad

Preparation Time: 10 min | Serving: 4 | Difficulty Level: Easy

Nutritional Info: Fat: 4.3g | Carbs: 3g | Protein: 5g

Ingredients

- 2 heads romaine lettuce

- Olive oil (for brushing)

- ¾ cup quartered cherry tomatoes

- ½ cup of corn

- ½ cup crumbled goat cheese

- 1 avocado, sliced

- 2 tbsp. lemon juice, freshly squeezed

- 2 tbsp. red wine vinegar

- ¼ tsp. salt

- ½ tsp. Dijon mustard

- ¼ cup olive oil

Steps for preparation

1. Preheat the grill until it reaches medium-high heat. Brush the surface of the romaine lettuce leaves with some olive oil and grill for about 4-5 minutes, turning them occasionally. Then, place the lettuce leaves on the salad plate and top them with the tomatoes, avocado, corn, and goat cheese.

2. Drizzle the dressing over the food and serve.

    FOR THE DRESSING:

3. In a bowl, whisk together the red wine vinegar, lemon juice, salt, mustard, and olive oil.

3. Grilled Peaches with Yogurt and Brown Sugar

Preparation Time: 15 min | Serving: 4 | Difficulty Level: Easy

Nutritional Info: Fat: 3g | Carbs: 8.9g | Protein: 6g

Ingredients

- Two peaches

- 2 tsp. melted butter

- 2-4 tsp. brown sugar blend

- ¼ cup vanilla yogurt

Steps for preparation

1. Preheat the grill until it reaches medium-high heat. Cut the peaches in half and remove the pits.

2. Brush the peaches with some melted butter and place them skin-side down on the heated grill.

3. Cook them for 4 to 5 minutes and flip them over once they start becoming tender.

4. Sprinkle some of the brown sugar on the peaches.

5. Once the sugar caramelizes, remove from the grill and let them cool.

6. Serve immediately.

4. Grilled Sirloin Salad

Preparation Time: 20 min | Serving: 4 | Difficulty Level: Easy

Nutritional Info: Fat: 8.7g | Carbs: 22g | Protein: 30.4g

Ingredients

- 1 tbsp. chili powder

- 2 tsp. dried oregano

- 1 tsp. dried thyme

- ½ tsp. salt

- ½ tsp. onion powder

- ½ tsp. garlic powder

- ¼ tsp. black pepper

- Sirloin steak, trimmed

- 8 cups of salad greens

- 1½ cups red bell pepper, cut into strips

- 1 cup red onion, sliced

- 1 tbsp. fresh parsley, chopped

- 1 tbsp. red wine vinegar

- 1 tsp. olive oil

- 1 tsp. fresh lemon juice

- 1 can whole-kernel corn, drained and rinsed

Steps for preparation

1. Combine the first seven ingredients together. Then, proceed to rub the spices onto the sides of the steak. Heat the nonstick grill pan over medium-high heat.

2. Then, place the steak on the pan and cook for 5 minutes on each side or until the meat reaches the desired degree of doneness. Cut the steak across the grain into thin slices.

3. While the steak cooks, combine the salad greens and remaining ingredients in a large bowl. Toss well to coat. Then, top with the steak and serve.

5. Chicken Teriyaki Drumsticks with the Tropical Fruit Salad

Preparation Time: 25 min | Serving: 4 | Difficulty Level: Easy

Nutritional Info: Fat: 9g | Carbs: 25g | Protein: 40g

Ingredients

- ¼ cup pineapple juice

- 3 tbsp. soy sauce

- 1 tbsp. light brown sugar

- 2 tsp. cornstarch

- Cooking spray

- 8 chicken drumsticks, skinned

- ¾ tsp. black pepper

- 1 cup fresh pineapple chunks

- 1 cup kiwi, peeled and sliced

- 1 cup halved fresh strawberries

- 1 tbsp. fresh cilantro, chopped

- 2 tbsp. lime juice

- ½ tsp. fresh ginger, peeled

Steps for preparation

1. In a shallow saucepan, whisk together the pineapple juice, brown sugar, soy sauce, and cornstarch over medium heat and wait for it to simmer. Then, cook it for 30 seconds, continuously stirring with a fork. Remove from the heat.

2. Place a grill pan over a medium-high flame and apply some cooking spray to it. Brush some oil on the chicken and sprinkle half a teaspoon of pepper over it. Place the chicken in the pan and cook it for 8 minutes, sometimes turning it over. Lower the heat and pour in some soy sauce. Allow the food to simmer for 15 minutes or until it is cooked, rotating and then brushing with the soy sauce mixture.

3. In a bowl, mix the remaining pepper, pineapple bits, strawberries, kiwi, cilantro, and ginger. Serve with the chicken and eat.

6. Grilled Cantaloupe Salad with Feta Cheese

Preparation Time: 15 min | Serving: 6 | Difficulty Level: Easy

Nutritional Info: Fat: 29g | Carbs: 18g | Protein: 9g

Ingredients

- 1 small shallot, diced

- 5 tbsp. champagne vinegar

- 1 tsp. honey

- 1½ tsp. salt

- Black pepper, to taste

- 5 tbsp. olive oil

- 1 cantaloupe, diced

- 1 English cucumber, sliced

- 6 oz. feta cheese, crumbled

- 3 oz. watercress

- 1 cup toasted hazelnuts, chopped

Steps for preparation

1. Preheat the grill until it reaches a high temperature of 500°F. Place the shallot and vinegar in a small bowl, allowing it to sit for 5 minutes. Now stir in the honey, salt, pepper, and oil.

2. Mix the cantaloupe and the remaining 1 tablespoon of oil in the large bowl. Place the cantaloupe on the oiled grates and allow it to roast uncovered until the grill marks appear, which should take around 2 to 3 minutes per side.

3. Transfer the grilled cantaloupe to the serving platter. Top it with some cucumber slices, feta cheese, and hazelnuts. Drizzle it with some vinaigrette and sprinkle the remaining salt on top.

4. Serve and enjoy.

7. Grilled Lamb Skewers with Warm Fava Bean Salad

Preparation Time: 15 min | Serving: 2 | Difficulty Level: Easy

Nutritional Info: Fat: 10.3g | Carbs: 23g | Protein: 24.8g

Ingredients

- 4 cups fava beans

- 1½ tsp. extra virgin olive oil

- 1 tbsp. fresh mint, chopped

- 1 tsp. grated lemon rind

- 2 tbsp. fresh lemon juice

- 1 tsp. salt

- ½ tsp. black pepper

- 2 tbsp. water

- 1½ lb. lamb leg, trimmed and cut into 1-inch cubes.

- Cooking spray

- 6 lemon wedges

Steps for preparation

1. Place some water in a pot and allow it to boil. Once it boils, pour the fava beans in the water for around 1 minute or until it gets tender. Then, drain the beans and rinse them with some cold water before draining once again. Remove the tough outer skin from the beans and discard the skins.

2. Combine and whisk together the olive oil, mint, lemon rind, lemon juice, salt, and black pepper in a medium-sized bowl. Heat 2 tablespoons of water in a saucepan over medium-high heat and add the beans to the pan. Cook them for 2 minutes or until the beans are completely hot. Now, add the beans to the juice mixture and toss them to coat.

3. Preheat the grill and apply some cooking spray to it.

4. Thread the lamb cubes onto skewers and spray them with cooking oil. Season the skewers evenly with the remaining salt and pepper. Place the skewers on the grill rack with the cooking spray and grill them for 7 minutes until the lamb is done. Continue to rotate them on occasion.

5. Serve with salad and lemon wedges.

8. Grilled Vegetable and Flank Steak Salad with Cheese Vinaigrette

Preparation Time: 30 min | Serving: 4 | Difficulty Level: Easy

Nutritional Info: Fat: 22.2g | Carbs: 8g | Protein: 28g

Ingredients

- 1 1 lb. flank steak, trimmed

- ¼ cup olive oil

- ½ tsp. garlic powder

- ¾ tsp. salt

- ½ tsp. black pepper

- 2 medium-sized yellow squash, halved lengthwise

- 2 ½-inch-thick red onion slices

- 1 red bell pepper, quartered

- 1½ tbsp. white wine vinegar

- Sugar

- 1 oz. blue cheese, crumbled

- ½ cup halved grape tomatoes

Steps for preparation

1. Warm the grill until it reaches medium-high heat.

2. Add garlic powder, oil, salt, and a pinch of pepper to the meat. Proceed to coat the steak with oil and place it in a pan. Cook the meat on either side for 4 minutes before removing and placing it on a cutting board.

3. Allow it to rest and then cut it.

4. Serve immediately.

9. Grilled Chicken Salad

Preparation Time: 15 min | Serving: 4 | Difficulty Level: Easy

Nutritional Info: Fat: 2.2g | Carbs: 23.6g | Protein: 14.7g

Ingredients

- 2 chicken breasts, halved

- 4 stalks of celery, chopped

- 1 large red bell pepper, diced

- ½ red onion, diced

- 1 can sweet corn, drained

- ¼ cup barbeque sauce

- 2 tbsp. fat-free mayonnaise

Steps for preparation

1. Preheat the grill until it is quite hot and brush some oil over it.

2. Grill the chicken on each side for 12 minutes or until the juices are visible on the surface.

3. In a large bowl, mix the chicken with the celery, red bell pepper, diced onion, and maize.

4. Finally, mix the barbeque sauce with mayonnaise in a small bowl and add it to the chicken and vegetables. Use some chilli to garnish and serve hot.

5. In another bowl, mix the squash, onion pieces, and bell pepper together. Stir in the oil, salt, and pepper.

6. Arrange the vegetables on the grill and cook them for four minutes. Stir them around and allow them to simmer for 2 minutes. Cut them into bite-sized pieces.

7. Combine the remaining two tablespoons of oil, a pinch of salt, pepper, sugar, butter, and vinegar together. Divide the tomatoes and vegetables into 4 bowls. Drizzle the vinaigrette over the veggies. Then, cut the steak into thin slices and divide the pieces between the 4 bowls.

10. Pasta Salad and Grilled Chicken

Preparation Time: 15 min | Serving: 4 | Difficulty Level: Easy

Nutritional Info: Fat: 13.2g | Carbs: 48g | Protein: 46.5g

Ingredients

- 4 skinless, boneless chicken breasts, halved

- Steak seasoning, to taste

- 8 oz. rotini pasta

- 8 oz. mozzarella cheese, cubed

- 1 red onion, chopped

- 1 head chopped romaine lettuce

- 6 cherry tomatoes, chopped

Steps for preparation

1. Preheat the grill until it reaches a high temperature. Then, proceed to season both chicken breast pieces with steak seasoning.

2. Add some oil to the grill. Then, grill the chicken pieces for 8 to 10 minutes along each side. Remove them from the heat and let them cool. Then, cut them into strips. Meanwhile, allow some water to boil in a pot on the stove. Then, place the rotini pasta inside the pot, add some salt to it, and let it boil for 10 minutes or until it finishes cooking.

3. Drain completely and rinse with cold water. Then, in a large-sized bowl, combine the cheese with the onion, lettuce and tomatoes. Finally, mix in the pieces of chicken and pasta. It's now ready to serve.

11. Grilled Chicken Wonton with Salad

Preparation Time: 20 min | Serving: 6 | Difficulty Level: Easy

Nutritional Info: Fat: 63g | Carbs: 50.7g | Protein: 32.6g

Ingredients

- 4 6-oz. chicken breasts, halved

- 2 tbsp. teriyaki marinade

- 8 green chopped onions

- 1 tsp. salt

- 1 tsp. pepper

- ½ cup sugar

- ¾ cup rice vinegar

- 1 cup olive oil

- 7 oz. pack wonton wrappers

- Half a cup frying oil

- 1 head iceberg lettuce

- 4 oz. water chestnuts, drained and sliced

- ¼ cup sesame seeds, toasted

- ½ cup sliced almonds, toasted

- 1 10-oz. mandarin orange segments, drained

Steps for preparation

1. Place the chicken breast pieces in a bowl and cover them with teriyaki sauce. Then, let the mixture marinate for 2 hours in the refrigerator.

2. Preheat your outdoor grill.

3. Then, put the onions, pepper, salt, sugar, olive oil, and rice vinegar in a blender to make the dressing. Now, blend everything until it is smooth, pour the contents in a small bowl, and refrigerate.

4. Grill the chicken, regularly flipping it until it is fully cooked. Place it on a cutting board and allow it to rest. Then, slice it into thin strips.

5. Place some oil in a large-sized skillet and allow it to heat up over a medium-high flame. Break the wanton wrappers into small strips and fry them until they are crispy. Then, move them onto a few paper towels to absorb any excess oil.

6. In a wide cup, mix the spinach, water chestnuts, sesame seeds, and sliced almonds together. Then, add the mandarin oranges and pour the dressing over the salad. Toss it gently and top with the roasted chicken strips and fried wontons.

12. Grilled Corn and Bell Pepper Salad

Preparation Time: 25 min | Serving: 6 | Difficulty Level: Easy

Nutritional Info: Fat: 9.2g | Carbs: 14g | Protein: 4g

Ingredients

- 2 large ears of corn
- 1 medium-sized red bell pepper
- 1 medium-sized yellow bell pepper
- 1 medium-sized shallot, peeled
- 3 tbsp. parsley, chopped
- 2 tbsp. olive oil
- 1 tbsp. apple cider vinegar
- ¼ tsp. salt
- ¼ tsp. black pepper
- ¾ oz. crumbled cottage cheese

Steps for preparation

1. Preheat the grill to 455°F.

2. Brush some oil over the grill and add the vegetables. Proceed to cook the corn for 15 minutes, rotating it every 5 minutes.

3. Cook the bell peppers for about 10 minutes, flipping periodically. Then, cook the shallot for 6 minutes. Remove the vegetables from the grill and allow them to cool for 5 minutes.

4. Chop the corn kernels from the cob and put them in a dish. Cut the bell peppers into 1/4-inch pieces. Then, proceed to chop the shallots and add the parsley, oil, vinegar, salt, and black pepper to the mixture. Mix everything together and sprinkle some cheese on top.

13. Souvlaki Chicken Salad

Preparation Time: 20 min | Serving: 4 | Difficulty Level: Easy

Nutritional Info: Fat: 32.3g | Carbs: 13.9g | Protein: 26.8g

Ingredients

- 1 tbsp. olive oil

- 1 tbsp. Greek seasoning

- 1 tbsp. lemon juice

- 2 garlic cloves, minced

- 1 lb. chicken breasts

- 6 tbsp. tzatziki sauce

- 2 tbsp. olive oil

- 2 tbsp. fresh lemon juice

- Pinch of salt

- 1 head of romaine lettuce

- ½ cup red bell pepper

- ½ English cucumber, sliced

- 8 oz. cherry tomatoes, halved

Steps for preparation

1. In a glass bowl, mix 2 tablespoons of olive oil, some Greek seasoning, 1 tablespoon of lemon juice, and garlic together. Now, add the chicken to the marinade and mix it together. Leave it to marinate in the fridge for about 2 hours, but not longer than 5 hours.

2. Mix the tzatziki with 2 tablespoons of olive oil and lemon juice, before seasoning with salt.

3. Preheat the outdoor grill to high heat and lightly brush oil on the grate.

4. Now, place the chicken slices over the grill and cook them for about 4 minutes. Turn the sides and grill until the center is no longer pink,

5. To confirm that the chicken is fully cooked, insert a thermometer into the center, which should read about 165° F (75° C).

6. In a small salad bowl, combine the romaine lettuce, bell pepper, cucumber, and cherry tomatoes. Sprinkle some tzatziki dressing over the vegetables and toss gently. Then, divide the salad into 3 equal parts and top it with the cooked chicken.

14. Amy's Sensational Summer Salad

Preparation Time: 20 min | Serving: 6 | Difficulty Level: Medium

Nutritional Info: Fat: 31.4g | Carbs: 35.5g | Protein: 22.2g

Ingredients

- 3 chicken breasts, halved

- 1 cup salad dressing

- 1 Granny smith apple

- 2 tbsp. lemon juice

- 1 head romaine lettuce, chopped

- 1 avocado, diced

- 4 oz. feta cheese, crumbled

- 1 ½ cups fresh strawberries, diced

- 1 cup dried cranberries

- ¾ cup balsamic vinaigrette

Steps for preparation

1. Place the chicken breast pieces and salad dressing in a plastic bag. Now, mix them well until the chicken pieces are coated with the dressing. Then, squeeze the air out of the bag and tightly seal it, before inserting it in the fridge to marinate.

2. Preheat the outdoor grill until it reaches medium-high heat and lightly brush it with oil.

3. Take the chicken out of the fridge and shake the pieces to remove any excess sauce. Grill the chicken pieces for about 4 minutes on each side, until they are no longer pink in the center or their internal temperature reaches about 165° F (75° C). Set them aside to cool as you prepare your salad ingredients.

4. In a large-sized bowl, mix the apple with some lemon juice and then drain the lemon juice.

5. Place the vegetables in a small mixing bowl and add some pepper, the chicken, diced avocado, cheese, strawberries, and cranberries. Add the balsamic vinegar and toss the salad gently.

6. Serve immediately.

15. Grilled Seasonal Fruit with Chicken Salad

Preparation Time: 15 min | Serving: 6 | Difficulty Level: Medium

Nutritional Info: Fat: 46g | Carbs: 23.2g | Protein: 17.8g

Ingredients

- 1 lb. boneless chicken breasts

- ½ cup pecans

- 1/3 cup red wine vinegar

- ½ cup white sugar

- 1 cup vegetable oil

- ½ onion, minced

- 1 tsp. ground mustard

- 1 tsp. salt

- ¼ tsp. ground white pepper

- 2 heads of lettuce

- 1 cup fresh strawberries, sliced

Steps for preparation

1. Preheat the outdoor grill until it reaches high heat.

2. Lightly brush the grill with the oil. Then, put the chicken pieces on the grill and allow the pieces to cook for 10 minutes on each side. Remove the chicken from the grill and allow it to rest. Then, cut the chicken into slices.

3. In the meantime, place the pecans in a clean and dry skillet over low heat. Cook the pecans until they are moist, constantly stirring them for around 8 minutes. Turn off the heat and set the pan aside.

4. Now, pour some red wine vinegar and olive oil in the blender, further adding the mustard, salt, and pepper. Now, blend everything together until it's smooth.

5. Then, place the lettuce on the serving pan and cover with roasted chicken strips, strawberries, and pecans. Drizzle some of the dressing over the dish and serve.

16. Grilled Chicken, Peach, and Arugula Salad

Preparation Time: 15 min | Serving: 6 | Difficulty Level: Medium

Nutritional Info: Fat: 13.2g | Carbs: 5.8g | Protein: 16.5g

Ingredients

- 5 tbsp. olive oil

- 1 tbsp. balsamic vinegar

- 1 tbsp. shallot, chopped

- 1 tsp. Dijon mustard

- ½ tsp. salt

- 4 peaches, halved and pitted

- 4 skinless chicken breasts, halved

- 8 cups baby arugula

Steps for preparation

1. Heat the outdoor grill until it becomes very hot and spray it with some oil. Whisk together 1/4 cup of oil, balsamic vinegar, Dijon mustard, shallots, and around 1/4 teaspoon of salt in a bowl.

2. Rub ½ a teaspoon of olive oil over the peaches, which should be cut in half.

3. Place the peaches face-down on the grill and roast them for around 5 minutes or until they are well cooked. Move the peaches onto a plate.

4. Brush the remaining oil over both sides of the pieces and salt to taste.

5. Cook the chicken on the grill for around 5 minutes per side.

6. Wash some arugula and divide it evenly between the plates, topping it with some peaches and the leftover chicken pieces.

Chapter 7: Miscellaneous

1. Grilled Herb and Cheese Stuffed Mushrooms

Preparation Time: 15 min | Serving: 4 | Difficulty Level: Easy

Nutritional Info: Fat: 12g | Carbs: 23g | Protein: 8g

Ingredients

- 4 large Portobello mushrooms

- ¼ cup panko breadcrumbs

- 1 tbsp. thyme, finely chopped

- 1 tbsp. oregano, finely chopped

- 2 tsp. rosemary, finely chopped

- 1 clove garlic, minced

- Salt

- Black pepper

- 1 oz. pimentos, chopped

- 1 tbsp. olive oil

- 2 tbsp. butter

- ¼ cup cheddar cheese (grated)

Steps for preparation

1. Wash the mushrooms and cut off the stems. Reserve the caps and finely chop the stems.

2. Mix together the breadcrumbs, thyme, oregano, rosemary, mushroom stems, garlic, salt, and pepper.

3. Pulse the mixture 15 times in the processor.

4. Stir in the pimentos.

5. Preheat the grill on medium-high heat and add some oil to the grill.

6. Brush the mushroom caps with olive oil and add 1/2 a teaspoon of butter to the inside of the cap.

7. Place the mushroom caps on the grill for 4 minutes.

8. Remove them from the grill, stuff with the breadcrumb mixture, and top with the grated cheese.

9. Return the mushroom caps to the grill and cook them for 4 minutes.

10. Remove them from the heat and allow them to rest for 5 minutes. Cut them into pieces and serve.

2. Grilled Portobello-Goat Cheese Pitas

Preparation Time: 15 min | Serving: 4 | Difficulty Level: Easy

Nutritional Info: Fat: 8.5g | Carbs: 39.8g | Protein: 11.9g

Ingredients

- 1 ½ tsp. garlic, minced

- 1 tsp. olive oil

- 4 6-inch pita pieces

- ½ tsp. salt

- ¼ tsp. black pepper

- 1 package of Portobello mushrooms

- Medium tomatoes, thick slices

- 1/3 cup goat cheese

- ½ cup fresh basil, chopped

Steps for preparation

1. Preheat the grill pan to medium-high heat.

2. Then, combine the garlic and oil and brush the mixture evenly over the pita bread pieces. Sprinkle a pinch of salt and pepper on the bread and place them in a pan to toast lightly.

3. Sprinkle a bit of salt and pepper evenly on the mushrooms and tomatoes. Place the mushrooms in the pan and cook them for 6 minutes or until they are tender, stirring them once. Remove the mushrooms from the pan and add the tomatoes, allowing them to cook for 1 minute.

4. Spread the goat cheese evenly on the pitas, then add the mushrooms and tomatoes. Finally, top with the chopped basil.

5. Serve.

3. Grilled Tofu Skewers

Preparation Time: 15 min | Serving: 4 | Difficulty Level: Easy

Nutritional Info: Fat: 9g | Carbs: 4g | Protein: 5g

Ingredients

Grilled tofu skewers:

- 1 350g block extra-firm tofu, drained and pressed for around 30 minutes

- 2 tbsp. soy sauce

- 2 tbsp. water

- 1 tbsp. maple syrup

- ½ tsp. smoked paprika

- ½ tsp. garlic powder

Spicy peanut sauce:

- ½ cup natural peanut butter

- ¼ cup coconut milk

- 2 tbsp. soy sauce

- 2 tbsp. lime juice

- 1 tbsp. Sriracha sauce

- ¼ tsp. garlic powder

Optional garnishes:

- Lime wedges

- 1 handful cilantro, roughly chopped

- 1 tbsp. roasted peanuts, roughly chopped.

Steps for preparation

1. Cut a block of tofu into eight long sticks.

2. Pour some soy sauce, water, and agave into a dish. Add some smoked paprika and garlic powder to the dish and mix together. Add the tofu to the mixture and leave it to marinate in the fridge for 30 minutes.

3. Mix all the ingredients of the sauce in a small bowl and store in the fridge.

4. Thread the tofu sticks onto the skewers. Then, heat the grill pan over medium-high heat and grill the skewers for around 10 to 15 minutes, turning them as needed until grill marks appear. Brush the skewers with the leftover marinade.

5. Remove and serve hot with peanut sauce.

4. Grilled Flatbread Chicken Curry

Preparation Time: 20 min | Serving: 4 | Difficulty Level: Easy

Nutritional Info: Fat: 15g | Carbs: 50g | Protein: 32g

Ingredients

- ½ cup carrots, peeled

- 2 tsp. ginger, minced

- ½ cup rice vinegar

- ¼ cup water

- 1 tsp. granulated sugar

- 1½ tsp. curry powder

- 1½ tbsp. olive oil

- ½ cup plain yogurt

- 2 tsp. honey

- ¼ tsp. salt

- 1 package of whole-grain naan

- 2 cups shredded chicken breast

- 2 oz. snow peas

- ¼ cup fresh cilantro leaves

- ¼ cup dry-roasted peanuts

Steps for preparation

1. In a normal-sized saucepan, add the carrot, ginger, vinegar, a quarter cup of water, and sugar and leave the contents to boil over a high flame. Cook them for 2 minutes and then remove from the heat, leaving it to cool.

2. In a medium-sized microwave dish, mix the curry powder with one teaspoon of oil. Now, microwave the mixture for around 50 seconds. Stir in the yogurt, honey, and some salt until the contents are blended together well.

3. Heat the grill and brush some oil onto the naan before adding it to the grill. Toast it for about 80 seconds on each side. Then, tear the naan in half and spread 1 tablespoon of the yogurt mixture on each half.

4. Drain the carrot mixture and place some of the carrots, chicken, peas, cilantro leaves, peanuts, and raisins on the naan. Drizzle some of the yoghurt on top of the naan and serve.

Conclusion

After completing this book and trying out many of the recipes, your skills will continue to improve and you will no longer remain a novice griller. You must continue practicing your grilling skills to ensure that they continue to improve so that you can eventually become a grilling expert!

Printed in Great Britain
by Amazon